Sermons From The Porch

Cycle C Sermons for the Second Half of the
Season After Pentecost
Based on the Gospel Lessons

Christopher Keating

CSS Publishing Company, Inc.
Lima, Ohio

SERMONS FROM THE PORCH

FIRST EDITION
Copyright © 2024
by CSS Publishing Co., Inc.

Library of Congress Cataloging-in-Publication Data

Names: Keating, Chris, author.
Title: Sermons from the porch : Cycle C sermons for the Sundays after
  Pentecost based on the gospel lessons : second half / by Christopher
  Keating.
Description: Lima, Ohio : CSS Publishing Company, Inc., 2024. | Includes
  bibliographical references.
Identifiers: LCCN 2024034196 | ISBN 9780788031212 (paperback)
Subjects: LCSH: Pentecost season--Sermons. | Communities--Religious
  aspects--Christianity. | Common lectionary (1992). Year C.
Classification: LCC BV4300.5 .K38 2024 | DDC 252/.64--dc23/eng/20240814
LC record available at https://lccn.loc.gov/2024034196

For more information about CSS Publishing Company resources, visit our website at www.csspub.com, email us at csr@csspub.com, or call (800) 241-4056.

e-book:
ISBN-13: 978-0-7880-3122-9
ISBN-10: 0-7880-3122-8

ISBN-13: 978-0-7880-3121-2
ISBN-10: 0-7880-3121-X

PRINTED IN USA

Dedication

To the saints of Woodlawn Chapel Presbyterian Church,
Wildwood, Missouri,
for their prayers and encouragement,
and to my amazing wife, Carol,
and wonderful children Katie (David),
Christine (Adam),
Cindy (Craig,)
and Dean,
and granddaughters Jacquelyn and Mia,
for the love we share and memories we treasure.

You are all God's front porch to me, and I cherish our life
together.

Contents

Introduction

You are somebody's front porch to God.
You are someone's doorway to mercy.
You are the world's threshold to kindness.
You are my entrance to letting go of regret.
No pressure, but…
Your life is a gateway to peace[1]
("You Are Somebody's Front Porch to God," by John Roedel used by permission)

Front porches are somewhat of an endangered species. Porches flourished through the eighteenth and nineteenth centuries but began losing their luster following World War II. While there is truth that the advent of air conditioning encouraged their disappearance, there were other factors at work as well. As Southern novelist Reynolds Price reminded us, front porches served more purposes than providing an escape from overheated interiors.[2] Their elimination from domestic architecture was the result of a changing culture.

Porches provided open spaces for family gatherings and story sharing. These rooms without walls became a hub for family learning as well as spaces for hospitality. They offered encounters with neighbors and with nature and were stages for performing the dramas of family life. They were incubators for courtships and romance, ground zero for the big firsts of relationships: dates, kisses, and engagements. At the other end of the life cycle, porches have served as the thresholds for encounters with grief, places for hugs, tears, and disbelief. Their open spaces provided front seat accommodations for witnessing the majesty of nature and all of her changing beauty.

Those events still occur, but the places where we watch or engage them have migrated elsewhere. Cars and air conditioning have caused some of these changes, but the truth is also that our passion for community life changed sometime after World War II. Television offered a new way of gathering, and a growing quest for greater autonomy

1. "You Are Somebody's Front Porch to God," by John Roedel. All rights reserved. Used by permission from the author.

2. Reynolds Price, "The Lost Room," in "Out on the Porch," (Chapel Hill, NC: Algonquin Books, 1992), p. 1.

and semi-anonymous individualism began replacing some of the traditions associated with life shared with others.

Yet those innate longings for community have remained despite attempts at being paved over by the steamrollers of individualism. We especially felt this during the pandemic, though wise congregations and their leaders had been feeling this disconnect for some time. Our reaction to the unjust deaths of Black persons such as Breonna Taylor and George Floyd prompted long-overdue conversations about racism. Locked down at home, we longed for places like a porch where stories could be swapped, jokes told, and lessons learned.

Our grandparents and great-grandparents used their porches for much more than a place of retreat from overheated houses. Front porch sitting cultivated a way of looking at the world, noting what was happening around you, and processing that input into learning. Backyard decks provide recreation and gathering space, but by and large these are private spaces. Some years ago, a friend and our son and I rebuilt our deck. Not long after we were done, my son started clipping back some invasive non-native plants that were drooping over the fence between our neighbor's yard and our yard. They stopped him, even though the branches were on our side and the plant is known to have a negative impact on Missouri gardens. "We like our privacy," our neighbor said, even though both of our decks look directly at each other.

Porches provided something a deck cannot supply. In reflecting on the front porch of his childhood home, Reynolds Price says that "all the urgent scenes…so many crucial similar scenes and lessons in my whole life and the lives I knew — not one of them could have happened indoors."[3] Their disappearance from our lives is likely unnoticed by many, but perhaps we do not know what we are missing.[4] In a survey of Southern writers Zora Neale Hurston, Gloria Naylor, and Randall Kenan, scholar Trudier Harris notes how those authors employed interpretative patterns of oral traditions common to porch sitting and porch listening. Harris says that the tasks of listeners included challenging speakers about details of familiar stories they overlooked. Such an interdependent relationship naturally enriched Southern literature. Harris noted: "southerners established and perpetuated

3. Price, *The Lost Room*, p. 11.

4. Quoted from https://xroads.virginia.edu/~CLASS/am483_97/projects/cook/first.htm, accessed 9/20/2023.

oral traditions with which the literature growing on that soil could not help be fertilizing."[5]

The wide-sweeping wrap around verandas of the south are our most common images of front porches, but architects note they were essential features to American homes across the country. Architect Davida Rochlin has written that "nobody thought much about the front porch when most Americans had them and used them. The great American front porch was just there, open and sociable, an unassigned part of the house that belonged to everyone and no one, a place for family and friends to pass the time."[6]

I have crystal-clear memories of sitting on the front porch of my grandparents' Chicago home. Their early twentieth-century home sat in the middle of a tree-lined block on Chicago's northwest side, not far from the Edgewater neighborhood. It was a concrete pad above street level that was abutted to their brick home. Street parking was limited in their neighborhood, which kept the sidewalks busy. Neighbors had to pass Grandma and Grandpa's middle of the block house on their way to shop at the Jewel, or catch the Clark Street bus, or head to church. My mom had been raised in this house, which was full of stories about family life during the Great Depression and World War II. Grandpa sat on the front porch in decent weather every morning, sipping coffee and reading the *Chicago Tribune*. Grandma would join him, often reading the weekly news from their hometown down state or tending to her crocheting. I loved running Matchbox cars in and out of the doors that connected the porch and living room, or even just sitting outside listening to my grandparents greet their neighbors.

There was a television inside, but it was rarely on. They switched it on for the nightly news and for a few afternoon soap operas, but most of their socializing happened outside. That home's porch has long since been enclosed, which probably provides a more useful cold-weather space. I doubt Grandpa ever thought about making it an indoor space. Their porch was integrated into their lives, offering a relaxing vantage point to watch the world.

When originally preached, the sermons in this collection were prompted by a desire to use the metaphor of a front porch as a tool for our church's summer faith formation. We hoped that a series of

5. Trudier Harris, *The Power of the Porch*, (Athens, GA: University of Georgia Press, 1996), p. xiii.

6. Davida Rochlin, quoted at https://xroads.virginia.edu/~CLASS/am483_97/projects/cook/first.htm, accessed 9/20/2023.

wide-ranging "front porch conversations" might help us integrate what was happening in our community with what was happening in our church. From there we began to see how the image of a front porch might help us create moments of hospitality, story-telling, and renewed engagement of faith.

We didn't replace our sanctuary chairs with rocking chairs — though that is not such a horrible idea. Instead, we imagined a space where both worship and conversations could occur in ways that provoked engagement with the community. We hoped to combine meeting others, storytelling, and prayer in ways that would lead to new growth.

As I remember it, my grandparents' porch was neither large nor elaborately furnished. There were a couple of old aluminum folding chairs set up against the brick front, and a few faded cushions. This was all that was needed to accommodate visitors. It wasn't outfitted with trendy objects or the latest designs. It was an informal, simple space that reminded Grandma and Grandpa that they were human beings, not human *doings*.

Across the street was the elementary school my mother had attended. By the 1960s, the school's changing demographics passed by their porch every morning and afternoon. I suspect a few of my grandparents' neighbors were suspicious of these newcomers. Many left the neighborhood for fancier suburbs where fenced-in back yards replaced front porches. The obvious point is that you can't pay attention to the changing world if you only see your own backyard.

I suppose my grandparents' porch intrigued me because front porches were not part of my suburban experience. We had front steps, not porches. Our backyards fulfilled some of those functions, especially when we lived in the east coast. We created community by hopping over fences for nightly conversations. Bolstered by milkcrates on either side of the fence, we hopped from yard to yard to play with friends. The longing for community moved from the front porch to backyard patios.

That ended when we moved to Southern California. Neighborhoods in suburban Los Angeles in the 1970s offered vestiges of front porches in the form of a front stoop. It was more of a border crossing than a porch. It was not a place for lingering conversation. In the backyard, a pink six-foot-tall cinder block wall surrounded the property, ensuring we retained control of who entered.

Front porches, on the other hand, offered less control. Arrivals were unpredictable, sometimes unannounced. They facilitated impromptu conversations with neighbors and offered early warning signs of intruding panhandlers and door to door solicitors. Sneak attacks by unwanted visitors could rarely be prevented. While the porch was also a border crossing, it was opened to the undomesticated realities around us.

In his memorable dystopian book, *Fahrenheit 451,* science fiction writer Ray Bradbury offered his own critique of vanishing porches. As his protagonist told the story, the loss of front porches was the result of an attempt to control conversations. "No front porches. My uncle says the architects got rid of the front porches because they didn't look well. But my uncle says that was merely rationalizing it; the real reason, hidden underneath, might be they didn't want people sitting like that, doing nothing, rocking, talking; that was the wrong *kind* of social life. People talked too much. And they had time to think. So, they ran off with the porches."

Whatever the reason, front porches have been replaced with elaborate outdoor living spaces complete with kitchens and outfitted with expensive furniture. They are intricately designed with televisions, LED lighting, and outdoor speakers. It's all a far cry from the mixed and matched folding chairs my grandparents owned. These new spaces are gorgeous but are symbols of individualism and an overall retreat from shared space.

Porch Church

All of this came to mind as our church began holding (metaphorical) summertime "Front Porch Conversations" following worship. We envisioned it as a place for conversation, a cool spot on a humid St. Louis summer day to share stories among all generations. We accommodated the air-conditioned generation by sitting inside. We hoped the novel name might encourage people to stick around, joking that "summer education hour" held no attraction at all. As it happened, the name stuck, and has grown to include a variety of summer activities, including worship themes and fellowship events.

There was something about "a front porch" conversation which made it sound as if it were a place where Atticus Finch or Scout might join us. We shortened worship a bit and made sure there was plenty of lemonade on hand. We used a bifocal approach to faith that involved listening to stories while seeing the needs of our neighbors up close.

Presbyterians being Presbyterians, we had previously believed that meetings and processes were the best way to encourage congregational innovation. But front porch conversations conveyed something much simpler. It became more than just a dressed-up title for a meeting. It became a friendly way to invite others to church, and an opportunity to create space for conversations. These conversations were helping us see the world in different ways, inviting us to step into the world where God is at work.

Our front porch functions as a transitional space, which is not a bad image for congregations of our time. Just as actual front porches were rooms without walls that merged a family's private world with the rest of the world, our front porch conversations bring us in touch with community leaders. I began to wonder about the role preaching might play in expanding the idea of sitting down on God's front porch.

Front Porch Preaching

The Luke texts for Cycle C are perfect front porch companions. The third gospel is replete with colorful characters, elaborate plots, and familiar stories, and striking themes. As a hermeneutical tool, the front porch invites us to encounter these stories in fresh ways. It's not hard imagining Luke inviting us to sit down in the shade of a broad veranda to pass the time of day by listening to these compelling stories. Stepping away from the heat and humidity of late summer day, these narratives offer us the chance to see where God is at work both in scripture and in our world. We're offered an opportunity to hear God's redemptive activity declared in Jesus' teachings and deeds. It empowers us to engage in our own context. These texts offer glimpses at all of Luke's unique features and theology, creating an ensemble cast of characters who will cause us to laugh, weep, smile, and reflect. As a public-facing theologian Luke offers a special concern for the marginalized and outcast that will challenge our own understandings of who belongs and who is excluded. The good doctor lets us peek at his world so that we might discern the ways God is at work today. We interact with these texts just as porch listeners interact with porch storytellers.

These lessons guide the church's transitions from summer into fall, inviting us into deep reflection about discipleship. We follow Jesus' move into Jerusalem, arriving shortly before Advent awakens new hope. On the way, we hear stories of stewardship, invitations to pray, and reminders of the surprising population of God's kingdom. We're invited to set a spell and to savor Jesus' words anew.

Each sermon is introduced with a brief exegetical reflection followed by the sermon ("Porch Talk"). The introductions are not meant to provide exhaustive exegesis. Instead, I've collected bits and pieces of conversations I've had not only with commentaries but with colleagues and parishioners that informed the sermon's direction.

My thanks to CSS Publishing and to David Runk and Tim Runk for their ministry of providing resources to pastors and congregations. Thanks as well to my church and staff members for their assistance and support. Special thanks to my family for your patience and encouragement. A heartfelt thanks is due to my writing teammates at *The Immediate Word* resource on CSS' SermonSuite.com: Mary Austin, Dean Feldmeyer, Elena Delhagen, Quantisha Mason-Doll, Katy Stenta, and Tom Willadsen. Our weekly conversations planted the seeds for these sermons. They may recognize some of their own ideas, for which I am extremely grateful.

Sit with these sermons and allow them to invite you to see the possibilities of where God is at work in your community. Come and sit for a spell on the front porch of Luke's Gospel and be challenged by an invitation to follow Christ. May your faithful response to what God is doing in your church and community grow like wisteria wrapping around the columns of a grand old porch, so that you may also become someone's front porch to God.

Proper 19 (24)
Luke 15:1-10

Lost In A Dime Store

There was a big crowd gathered around the porch this morning, and according to Luke the neighbors were not at all pleased. Luke 15 opened with throngs of tax collectors and sinners showing up to listen to Jesus, only to be met by the grumbling and grousing of the religious elites. "This fellow welcomes sinners and eats with them" (Luke 15:3). The grumbling led straight to a series of parables taken from Luke's lost and found department, all centered in the reminder that God seeks out those who have wandered. Luke's theological concerns for the outcasts and marginalized were prominent straight from the start. But while our eyes are directed to the tax collectors and sinners — indeed, who could be more lost than them — Luke may have been planning a little sleight of hand. Perhaps Luke was suggesting that the lost were none other than the ever-muttering adversaries of Jesus, the Pharisees, and teachers of the law.

It's a path worth traveling, but interpreters should use caution to avoid mischaracterizing Jewish groups in the New Testament. Reiterating tired stereotypes and anti-Jewish attitudes missed the point Luke was urging his listeners to see. Our tendency to characterize the Pharisees as hypocritical legalists missed the point. Instead of reinforcing old stereotypes, the porch preacher can probe a bit deeper: what is it that keeps us recognizing our own sense of being lost, mired in layers of tradition which no longer support us in loving both God and the neighbor?

Consider the different ways Luke used lostness as a theme. Chapter 15 introduced us to lost sheep, lost coins, and lost sons. Everything was lost, maybe even the remote control! Jesus' exploration of God's abundance stands in contrast to what has been lost. These texts offer evidence of Luke's theology of reversal. The hyperbole was evident: Jesus' description of God's provision may even feel a bit outsized or even outlandish. When Jesus asked which of you might abandon 99% of your income in pursuit of a 1% loss, we can imagine the crowd looking at each other and saying, "Well, I wouldn't do that!" But that seemed to be the point: the one who is lost shall be found. There's another side, too. What if the runaway sheep was the one who was practicing good self-differentiation by moving out of the herd-mentality of his siblings? What if that one sheep just needed some breathing room, or space to explore themselves? What sort of care is required for those who are left behind, who are angry and mad at the one who left? What are the risks involved for the shepherd? The text leaves so many questions. Why does being found leave so many feeling disturbed? In the end, the weight of these parables leads to an emerging question: in a world where lostness dominates, how do we experience the joy of being found today?

Porch Talk

I sprinted up the short flight of slate stairs outside the large home's understated front porch, knowing that this would be unlike any pastoral call I had ever made. I wasn't yet able to understand that across the world at probably the exact same time, thousands of pastors, rabbis, chaplains, religious leaders, and friends were doing the same thing. I was lost in a state of grief that had begun at 8:46 a.m. Eastern time when the first plane crashed into the World Trade Center. A phone call had brought me to the home of a church member whose brother worked in the North Tower. I pressed the doorbell, preparing to cross into a zone of lostness.

It was Tuesday, September 11, 2001. The brother of one of our church members, a rising star on Wall Street, was in his office on the 104th floor of Two World Trade Center when the planes crashed into the towers. He had managed to make a frantic call to his wife, from the 104th, but then all communication was lost. He was a 38-year-old executive, husband, father, and die-hard Cincinnati Bengals fan who wore orange Converse sneakers with tiger stripes painted on them every game day.[7] But before some of us had finished breakfast, he was gone.

In so many ways, we all fell to the ground lost that day. We experienced a profound sense of collectively being lost no one had ever experienced. We watched as smoke filled the streets of New York City, the corridors of Washington, DC, and a field outside Shanksville, Pennsylvania. Separated by miles and hundreds of thousands of unique stories, we were all united in our experiences of being lost.

7. Douglas MacMillan "Doug" Cherry, https://www.tumblr.com/sept11memori-
   als/32707048523/douglas-macmillan-doug-cherry-bengals-all-the

What had been a morning filled with everyday routines, cranky kids, and cups of coffee quickly transformed into heavy sighs and collective grief. Feeling lost is the only way I can describe those memories, even more than twenty years later.

We remember where we were that morning—at home, commuting to work, watching morning television, boarding airplanes. We might have been alone or in a crowd—but each of us felt as if we were profoundly lost. Familiar streets became a new and strange place. Part of us — nearly three thousand people — were gone, ripped from our world. More than two decades down the road, perhaps as many as a million more lives have been lost in the subsequent war on terrorism. We've become acclimated to taking off our shoes in airports and waiting in long screening lines. But some days we still feel lost.

"Think of that thing most precious in your life and what it would be like to lose it, whether through carelessness, or intent, or theft," writes Helen Montgomery Debevoise, "Something on which you place extreme value goes missing. You would be devastated. Not that you cannot continue; you can. People adapt—but life is incomplete. Part of the whole is missing."[8]

Being lost was on Jesus' mind that day. Luke gathered a trio of parables in chapter 15 to tell stories about a lost sheep, a lost coin, and a lost son. These stories are familiar to us, though that does not make them any less challenging. Jesus, Luke told us, has been whooping it up with the wrong crowd, and that has stoked the interest of those watching him — but not in a good way. Have you ever noticed that whenever the good, faithful religious people are interested in what Jesus is doing it is not because they approve?

They are grumbling because they do not approve of him eating with those who are sinners — tax collectors and swindlers who have defrauded others and embezzled their way to the top. The religious authorities are grumbling because they do not feel comfortable eating with "those" people. They do not deem it appropriate for Jesus to be hanging out with this sort of riffraff. "Those" people were not acceptable because they did not play by the rules.

It's pretty easy to imagine that the religious leaders assumed Jesus was referring to the sinners and tax collectors when he spoke of those who were lost. But that might not be entirely true. The truth is, as Lynn Japinga points out, "almost everyone can find a reason to grumble

8. Ibid.

about somebody. The reason for disapproval is not ritual purity but identity and beliefs."[9]

Perhaps the Pharisees were lost in their grumbling, much like anyone who persists in finding fault and disdain with others. We allow our grumbling to lead us down winding paths that usually guide us away from relationships of reconciliation. We grumble with those we disagree with or find disagreeable even on the most trivial matters. Half of our country cannot agree on whether sugary carbonated beverages should be called "soda" or "pop," or even "Coke." Maybe Jesus had another idea in mind, because, if truth be told, getting lost is not so hard. It's being found that gets tricky.

Anyone who has ever fumbled through unfamiliar city streets or owned a set of car keys knows how easy it is to get lost. I consider it a good day when I manage to keep track of my wallet and keys all day long. My children have suggested that I get Apple® air tags to find my other Apple® air tags. Maybe, just maybe, the point of these parables is not so much about who is lost as it is about being found, and the joy that comes as the one who is lost is restored into community.

As I said, losing things has never been a particular challenge for me. More than once, this has included losing my sense of direction, at least temporarily. It's not that I lack spatial awareness. Despite what my children will tell you, I actually have a great sense of direction. It's not foolproof, of course, and is rarely a match for my outsized sense of curiosity and willingness to explore. It is curiosity that led to an incident my children refer to as "The Night Dad Took Us to Look at Christmas Lights and Almost Got Us Murdered." (That is a gross characterization as far as I'm concerned. There was never a time when we were in any danger.) Our daughters were young, clad in Christmas pajamas, and bundled into car seats. Our quest for a certain neighborhood's highly regarded display went awry, however, and soon we ended up driving across an empty field. Nary was there any sign of Christmas lights. My one daughter told me she thought we'd all end up as the subject of a "Dateline" episode. I still think they were overreacting a bit.

But the truth is I do get distracted sometimes. I can identify with Jesus' stories of being lost because they remind of the times when

9. Joseph J. Clifford et al., "Proper 19 (Sunday between September 11 and September 17 Inclusive)," in *Connections: A Lectionary Commentary for Preaching and Worship: Year C: Season after Pentecost*, ed. Joel B. Green et al., First edition., vol. 3 (Louisville, KY: Westminster John Knox Press, 2019), 319.

curiosity has caused me to detour from the path I was traveling. There was a time, for example, that I managed to get lost in a dime store. Not a WalMart or Target, but an old dime store slightly smaller than a grocery store. Getting lost in a dime store was no mean trick, especially if you were shopping with my mother.

My mother was never one for long shopping trips. She moved quickly and purposefully, and never allowed me out of her focus. Managing to get out of her sight was nearly a job for Houdini. Added to this was the reality that in this particular store one could stand in the middle and clearly see the entire store. As mom and dad pointed out to me later, if I had simply looked up, I would have seen them. Whatever, I was lost.

Frankly, being lost felt special and kinda cool. Wandering among the aisles of cheap housewares and bowls of goldfish, a mix of fear and elation swept over me. On the one hand, I felt lost and abandoned, set adrift as an orphan in the world. (Being dramatic came easy for me.) Survival would depend on the kindness of strangers. Bereft of comfort as I may have been, at least I was surrounded by cheap candy and goldfish.

At the same time, I felt a strange sense of elation, even mastery. I would climb through his abyss and make it to the other side. There would be no need to call in Navy search and rescue teams, or even a squad of police officers and bloodhounds. I knew I wouldn't be lost long because I remembered the store had a public address system.

In my nine-year-old mind, the answer to being lost was asking the store employees to broadcast my name across the store. The thought of hearing them say my name over the PA system was true consolation. They would announce that I was lost, and in need of my parents to come claim me. The only thing better would be getting on television.

Unfortunately, my parents did not think so. While the shepherd rejoices when he finds the lost sheep, my parents were utterly embarrassed. "If you had just turned around you could have seen where we were standing," they told me as we rushed out of the store. I'm pretty sure we never went to that store again.

I wonder if the shepherd in Jesus' parable might have muttered something similar under his breath. Well, perhaps the shepherd would use more earthy vocabulary, but you get the idea. Ever have a dog charge the front door and take off through the neighborhood? I doubt that catching a runaway sheep is any easier. We're missing the backstory and other details, but it is not hard to imagine a paunchy, red-faced, middle-aged shepherd huffing and puffing his way as the lone lamb took off.

"If you would just stand still, I could take you home," he shouted. Meanwhile, the other 99 sheep were left alone to fend for themselves— literally, as Luke told us, they were out in the boonies by themselves.

But that is the good news hidden in this story: the shepherd, for whatever reason, acted irresponsibly by leaving the other 99 sheep behind to go searching for the one that was lost. That is filled with the loving compassion and determination of God that searched for those who were missing. The shepherd knew the flock was incomplete. Just as Jesus went out searching for those who were lost — lepers, tax collectors, outcasts, — this shepherd went searching for the one sheep.

It's not a decision many would choose. Imagine if Jesus was talking with business executives. He might ask them, "Which of you would leave the doors to your store wide open with 99% of your stock on the shelves while you go searching for the 1% of your product that was stolen?" No one would take that bet. Who would go searching for one sheep — just 1% of their herd—while leaving the others wide open to being attacked?

The answer is: not many. To be honest, few people would do that. You can't drop everything and go after the one that wandered away. I'm willing to guess that more than a few of Jesus' listeners would have shaken their heads in disbelief. The hill country where sheep were grazing were filled with dangers. Pursuing that one sheep while leaving the other unattended would not make a lot of sense.

Leaving the majority behind while you go searching for the minority has never played well in our culture. It is at the heart of resistance to dismantling racism, for example. Afraid to make white people uncomfortable, we perpetuate myths and stereotypes. In that sense, who are the ones who are truly lost?

It's true. Getting lost is not very hard. Any sheep can wander away. Any coin can roll behind the sofa. How many times do you lose a remote control, cell phone, glasses, or keys? But as Jesus told the story, the real trick is getting found. And this is where the story challenges us.

It challenges me to wonder about who is missing. Who has been excluded, or told they are not good enough to eat with Jesus? Who has been lost—caught in the rip tides of a confused and broken world, isolated, afraid, or alone? Who has been scolded into thinking they should not ask for help in being found? I am challenged by the reminder that God calls us to be passionate about loving those who feel they are lost. We do this not because we want the church to be filled on Sunday morning but because the God we worship calls us to go and to search for those who are lost and missing. We do this not to change them, not to force them to act in a certain way, but to share the joy that comes when the community is complete.

Getting lost is easy…but being found is another matter.

That is why being found is a matter of rejoicing — no matter how much the sheep fusses with being carried on the shepherd's shoulders. Being found is about God making sure nothing has been lost. The herd was incomplete without the lost sheep. The woman's bank account was less than it should be without the missing coin. There is great joy in these stories, not because the sheep comes to its senses and makes his way home, but because God knows something is missing.

Following 9/11, people realized something was missing — a person, a loved one who had died, or a gap in their life that could not be filled by something else. Many found their way back into church. This is what we learn by listening to Jesus: there is deep joy in know you have been found.

Amen.

The Dishonest Manager:
Clever, Shrewd, Crooked, Or Disciple?

Up on the porch this week comes the parable often called the parable of the unjust steward. But is that the correct title? Would it be better named the case of the shrewd steward? Parables can be deceiving, and this one is no different. It surprises us, and even its best answers are baffling. It seems that Jesus is applauding his dishonesty, which only confounds our imagination. Is Jesus suggesting that disciples should get into cahoots with organized crime? Should we take the weekly collection to the horse track, or hand it over to arbitrage dealers, making friends with the "mammon of wickedness?"[10]

Before we can interpret this parable, it is important to consider our focal point. What grabs our attention in this story? My friend and writing colleague Mary Austin once remarked that what looks dishonest from the point of privilege may look like survival for someone in need. From this point of view, the manager might have been simply trying to make ends meet.

Encountering this parable will look different depending on our own socio-economic status. Do we see it as a story of a dishonest manager who finally gets caught? Or do we value his street-smarts and ability to think on his feet? Does Jesus' call to "make friends of yourselves by means of dishonest wealth" offend or challenge? Meanwhile, particularly during fall stewardship season, are we open to discovering how our commitment to Christ is reflected in our attitudes toward money and possessions? Jesus offers us a chance to consider just what is at stake when it comes to managing something even larger and more valuable than treasure on earth.

Porch Talk

Not long before I graduated from college, the chair of the journalism department called me into her office. She told me she had heard that I

---

10. Luke T. Johnson, *Luke* (Collegeville, MN: The Order of St. Benedict, Michael Glazier Books, 1991, p. 243).

was forsaking a career in journalism for the ministry — and while she did not say it out loud, I could tell she was not completely enthusiastic about that plan. She certainly did not want to discourage me, she said, but she did want me to know her opinion about preachers in general, and Presbyterians in particular. At the top of the list, she said, was preaching about money.

She was clear: "Now I go to church every now and then, and if I think the sermon has been good I might put in a five-dollar-bill in the offering plate. But if the minister starts talking about money, then I get up and leave. Do you hear what I'm saying?"

I nodded politely, but her words stuck with me throughout seminary and well into my first church where I was serving as an associate pastor. As the senior pastor was giving me his orientation to the church, he looked me square in the eye and said, "You can preach about anything, but don't talk about money."

I found out the reason for his concern a few weeks later when I met an elderly gentleman at a community meeting. He asked what I did for a living, and I told him I was one of the pastors at First Presbyterian Church. "Oh, I used to go to that church," he told me, "But I stopped because of the building campaign. All the minister ever talked about was money." Even though I was a newbie at the church, I had heard some of the stories about the most recent building campaign that had concluded a couple of years ago. The funds were used to spruce up the fellowship hall and make it more usable for the church's current needs. Like many building projects, this one had been successful, but not without controversy. I was intrigued what about the building campaign had this man upset. "You didn't see the need for an updated fellowship hall?" I asked. "Fellowship hall?" he said, "What fellowship hall? I'm talking about the 1948 campaign to remodel the sanctuary."

Money creates long memories. Money creates memories of the early days of marriage when we were not smart enough to know how poor we were. Money creates memories of days when the paycheck would arrive ten days after the bills were due. Money fuels anxieties of never seeming to have enough but also the and the deeper satisfaction from squirreling away a little extra.

In the earliest days of our marriage, whenever I might get a call from a local funeral home to lead a service for someone without a church home, Carol and I would make the $25 honorarium stretch all week. One time when her parents were visiting, we took them to see a musical produced by a community theater company. On the way out of the theater, I turned to my mother-in-law and said, "Well, you can thank Mrs. Peabody for these tickets." Jackie, always on point with etiquette, turned to me and said, "Please send me her address." I winked at Carol and said, "Well, I can drive you by the cemetery on the way home if you'd like!"

We resist talking about money and wealth in church because we have been taught these are private matters. Yet much of the gospel, indeed much of scripture itself, is far from neutral when it comes to economics. Indeed, rather than avoiding the topic, time after time Jesus wades into the deep waters of conversations about money — not as a way of condemning wealth necessarily but instead as an indicator of what it means to dwell secure in God's provisions. His message takes clear aim at those who take advantage of the poor, or who squander the gifts they have been given.

But, like my professor reminded me, whenever a preacher starts talking about money, all sorts of warning lights start flashing. And that is especially true as we hear Jesus' words "You cannot serve God and wealth." They shock us, and arouse our suspicion, maybe even our guilt.

We wonder why Jesus doesn't stick to matters of salvation…and the answer is…he does. Time and time again, Jesus wandered into the thicket of human life. He was always concerned, as Walter Brueggemann observed, about the ways money and possessions are used in a world where God is in control.[11]

Pay attention to this tag line at the end of a confusing and enigmatic story. The first challenge in this story is deciding its title: is the manager clever, shrewd, crooked — or faithful?

Jesus' parable is a bit of a winding hike. In the space of a few verses, we meet a manager employed by a wealthy master. Having heard speculation and rumors about the slave — face it, that is what he was, a slave — the master called him into his office and demanded that he hand over the books. As the story reads in Clarence Jordan's *The Cotton Patch Gospels*, the master quizzed his servant about the bookkeeping. "Let me have your accounts so I can see if you can be manager around here any longer."[12]

11. Walter Brueggemann, Interpretation Bible Resources: Money and Possessions (Westminster John Knox, 2019), 199.

12. Clarence Jordan, *The Cotton Patch Gospel* (Macon, GA: Smyth & Helwys Pub., 2004), Lk 16:1.

What to do? In a moment of clarity, the slave considered his options. It's one of the more honest lines of scripture: "I'm not strong enough to dig ditches and I'm too ashamed to beg." He had to come up with a plan to deal with the master's treasure.

The story then took another wild turn as the manager—already accused of cooking the books — decided to put them back on the boiler. He called the debtors into his office, got what he could, then closed the accounts.

Once again, hear Clarence Jordan's rendering of these words from the *Cotton Patch Gospels*. "I'll fix it so that when I'm fired as manager his creditors will still welcome me into their places of business.' He called up each one of his boss' customers and said to the first home, 'How much do you owe my boss?" He replied, "I owe him for 900 gallons of oil." "All right," said the manager, "we'll settle the account if you'll sit right down and write us a check for 450 gallons. Okay?" Then he said to another, "How much do you owe?" He replied, 'For 1,000 bushels of wheat." The manager said, 'Just write us a check for 800 in full settlement."

"And the boss," says Jesus, "gave the crooked manager credit for pulling such a slick trick."[13]

What on earth was Jesus suggesting? He praised actions that are an affront to our sensibilities—who would commend a cheat or an embezzler? What church accountant would approve an exchange like that? Yet, Jesus commended the dishonest servant. It makes me wonder, was this man shrewd, clever, or crooked? Or, rather, was he a disciple?

Read the parable carefully, and the answer becomes clear.

First, it is entirely possible to translate the phrase "charges were brought" as "falsely accused." These accusations may have been nothing more than a whisper campaign against the servant, or they could have been true. Either way, the guy realizes that he needs to do something quickly because he's about to lose his job.

Secondly, there's the word "squandered." It's a great word. It speaks of recklessness and thoughtless selfishness. Jesus used this word one other time in the gospel when he told the story of the prodigal son. The wastefulness of the son was mirrored by the false accusations of the manager.

13. Ibid.

The prodigal squandered his father's resources. In this case, the servant was falsely accused of squandering resources. It makes me wonder — who else in this story would be falsely accused of wasting the gifts of God?

Jesus — and later, the disciples. And even later, the apostles as they were sent into the world. Some would grumble and complain about how the money was spent; how the resources were used. Some would drum up false accusations against Jesus, the disciples, and the church. No wonder Jesus praised the servant: for whoever was faithful in a very little is faithful also in much.

Moreover, his failure was also a sign of something more concerning. It seems Jesus was reminding us that the pursuits of the kingdom are even more pressing, even more vital, than clinging to earthly possessions.

Was he crooked, clever, or shrewd? Perhaps we might say that the guy was "creatively faithful."

There are plenty of times in our journey of faith where we do not think we will have enough — sometimes that will be faith, sometimes that will be energy, sometimes that will be money. And while I do not advocate for the church to create Ponzi schemes for making money, I do believe Jesus was suggesting that the servant depended completely on the gracious mercy of the master. The servant knew that faith must propel him into action. It was a leap of faith.

He was not crooked; he was a wise disciple. He acted decisively, shrewdly, and energetically. The lesson I hear for me in this is that the treasure entrusted to us –family, career, gifts, and yes, our money, we are called not to be faithless and scared, but creative, faithful, and shrewd, for none of us can serve two masters.

There's grace in this story. Jesus reminded the disciples that wealth was a gift to be managed according to the priorities of the gospel. The life of a disciple, wrote Fred Craddock, was one of faithful attention to the frequent and familiar tasks of each day. But Jesus' words, said Craddock, seemed to offend Christians who thought Jesus was commending dishonesty.[14] But, said Craddock, Jesus' words remind us that the task of discipleship is to pay attention to the "frequent and familiar tasks of each day." Craddock's wisdom remains true today. "The one faithful in today's nickels and dimes is the one to be trusted with the big account," he writes, "but it is easy to be indifferent toward small

14. Fred Craddock, "Luke" Interpretation Commentary series, Luke 16:1-13 (electronic version).

obligations while quite sincerely believing oneself fully trustworthy in major matters.[15]"

"Whoever is faithful in a very little is faithful also in much." That is the point, said Jesus. One of my heroes of the faith, the Reverend Doctor William Robert McClelland, was once asked, "Bob, should the church accept tainted money?" Bob replied, "The only problem with tainted money is that there's 'taint enough of it!" He was probably exaggerating. Yet he reminds me of Jesus' point: do not worship wealth and God but instead understand how God uses our everyday treasure to offer others the hope of the kingdom.

Amen.

15. Fred B. Craddock, *Luke*, Interpretation, a Bible Commentary for Teaching and Preaching (Louisville, KY: John Knox Press, 1990), 191–192.

Proper 21 (26)
1 Timothy 6:6-19, Luke 16:19-31

Haunted By Haughtiness

Luke's parable of Lazarus and the Rich Man (who was sometimes called "Dives,") continued Jesus' instructions to the disciples about money. Luke was the only gospel-writer to include this parable, which was consistent with Luke's concern for the poor. Allowing Lazarus and the rich man to stand on the porch brought them into the same space yet did not resolve the tension that existed between these two characters.

Issues related to wealth and poverty are primary concerns for Luke, proving to be every bit as challenging to contemporary audiences as they might have been to original listeners. Last week's enigmatic parable (Luke 16:1-13) is separated from this week's parable by an interlude of three sayings in verses 14-18 which seem to vilify the Pharisees. It's easy to sit on the porch and wag fingers at the Pharisees' hypocrisy, but there is danger in falling into that age-old trap. As Amy Jill Levine and others have observed, these sort of Pharisee-bashing has contributed to a long-history of promoting Jewish hatred.[16] Levine and others have urged caution in carefully evaluating a more accurate view of the Pharisees that does not promote anti-Jewish bias.

This week's parable is a yet another reminder of how easily power and privilege can blunt our perspective. The wealthy man was unable to see the injustice perpetrated on Lazarus. It's interesting to note that Lazarus was the only character in Jesus' parables who was named. It's a subtle clue, perhaps a way of reiterating God's explicit care for those who had suffered so much earthly harm. Luke was naming God's provision for the man who had so little but suffered so much. The critique of the privileged was unflinching. Even after his death the rich man was unable to perceive the inequities that caused Lazarus' suffering. As far as the rich man was concerned, Lazarus existed only to serve his needs. It begs questions of how wealthy we are in our acts

---

16. See, for example, "Preaching and Teaching the Pharisees," by Amy-Jill Levine, pp. 403-427, in *The Pharisees*, Joseph Sievers and Amy-Jill Levine, eds., Eerdmans Publishing, (Grand Rapids, MI), 2021.

of compassion, and what is needed for balancing the great (and ever-widening) chasms between rich and poor in today's world.

Porch Talk

The first summer we were married, I worked in the mailroom of Princeton University's library. I took the job because (a) I needed a job and (b) I figured that would be as close as I would ever come to being inside an Ivy League college. Both things turned out to be true.

The mailroom was fascinating. My coworkers included a chatty retired mail carrier with a genuine upbeat personality. Across from us worked a guy whose gray ponytail and leather jackets gave off hitman vibes. If this had been the set of the Sopranos, I could have been sitting in the back of a butcher shop with Paulie Walnuts and Richie Aprile. It was, after all, New Jersey. Everything of importance flowed through the mailroom: rare books, research volumes to the physics lab, envelopes stuffed with hefty donations, and even the occasional billionaire like Malcolm Forbes who preferred to come in through the loading dock so he wouldn't be seen.

All of this was the purview of the mailroom manager, a guy not much older than me who was just trying to figure out what he wanted in life. I could tell it was going to be a fascinating summer. It was in that mailroom that I learned a powerful lesson about humility. Every week the university's trash haulers would back up into the loading dock, empty the trash and drive away. One day the boss of the mailroom started an argument with the trash guys. It quickly escalated into a bigger disagreement. The next thing I knew I heard the boss say, "Well, what do you know? You're just a garbage man." Things got very quiet. The driver looked at our boss and shook his head, "Yeah, you're right, I'm just a garbage man, and you're just a mail room manager. I work hard and am proud of what I do." The trash guy nodded his head and backed the truck out of the dock. Decades later, that event is still seared into my mind.

The chasm between the loading dock and the garbage truck was deep. For all anyone knew, the truck driver and the mailroom manager could have both been making equal salaries. But a great and deep chasm was fixed between them. My boss was unwilling to admit that he was not seeing the entire picture.

Our world is filled with gaps and chasms. There are gaps between age groups and deep divides within politics. We live in a time when the division between rich and poor, between races, between countries. The chasm between the wealthiest Americans and the poorest Americans is greater than it ever has been, even in a time when incomes are growing. There are educational gaps, learning gaps...there are gaps between actual economic output and potential economic outputs...our world is filled with more canyons and chasms than Zion National Park.

Jesus' world, too, was filled with gaps. And while we might find it hard to relate to either the haughty rich man or the emaciated and starving Lazarus, we do know something about gaps, canyons, and caverns.

When I was young our family took a driving vacation across Utah and Colorado. It was not until that vacation that I knew my mother was terrified of canyons—especially when they were twelve inches outside the door of your car. My mother was as strong and independent woman as I have ever known, but five minutes inside Bryce Canyon or Zion National Park, and she was huddled below the dashboard, completely panicked by the canyons that were passing by our window.

We may hold the world's record for the least amount of time ever spent in Zion National Park.

Jesus' story in Luke 16:19-31 is a story about minding the gap, as they might say in England. He told us a story of two people who lived in close proximity to each other, but whose lives were divided by as deep and treacherous a gap as one could ever imagine. There was, indeed, a fixed chasm between the rich man and Lazarus, but not just in death.

The two of them lived their entire lives within feet of each other, though they never really knew just how close they were.

"There was a rich man, dressed in purple and fine linen," Jesus told us. Immediately we're thrown off balance because, like my old boss in the mailroom, we can quickly say, "He's not like me at all."

That is true. In fact, neither of the characters in this little story bear much resemblance to our lives, neither the rich man with the over inflated ego or the desperately poor Lazarus who cannot even manage to raise his head off the ground bear much resemblance to any of us, rich or poor.

The challenge of the story is looking beyond the immediate characters in order to see the invisible forces that pushed them apart.

The rich man was dressed in purple clothing, the sort of garments reserved for the elitest of the elite, the most powerful royal families. Few people had the resources to live in a house with gates. These clues tell us he was not only rich, but *very* rich, fully absorbed in his own privilege and status. Jesus was trying to tell us, "He's not an ordinary guy."

But, as Amy Jill Levine. Levine pointed out in her book *Short Stories By Jesus*, we are not exactly like the poor man, either. While the contrast between the two of them couldn't have been starker, it is also clear that there's a gap between us and Lazarus. We do not live in a billionaire's penthouse, but neither are we lying in the filth of the streets. We do not live in the gutters, nor do we live in the glittery atmosphere of the rich man — a man whose ego seemed to be even larger than his bank balance.

The truth is, we're unaccustomed to either extremes Jesus described in this story. Neither the rich man, whom legend has assigned the name "Dives" because of the Latin mistranslation of the word "rich," nor Lazarus (whose name means "God helps") are part of our frame of reference.

Because of this, it might be easy to dismiss this parable as either being irrelevant or an overdone morality tale. Yet, as the parable draws us into the story, we see ourselves refracted in the prism of God's abundance. Jesus called us to see the meaning of this story as it flowed from his own life, death, and resurrection. Mary Hinkle Shore helpfully pointed out that Jesus was telling us a story that reminds us of the ways his life, death, and resurrection provided the bridge across the gaps of the world. Jesus told us a story with these nearly ridiculously highly caricatured individuals and invited us to see the rather poor job we have done in minding the gap.

The rich man, Dives, had failed, in Paul's words, to know there "is great gain in godliness combined with contentment." His life had been one of constant motion; a driving force always seeking more...more things, more control, more power, more wealth. He was haunted by his own haughtiness and self-indulgent ego.

He was the one who had cut himself off from the poor of the land. He was the one who had constructed fences to keep poor people like Lazarus off his property. He was blinded by pride — not the healthy sort of pride that gives thanks for blessings, but the haughty, arrogance that believed not only was he better than others, he simply did not need anyone else.

Jesus was telling us, "Mind the gap."

It's a lesson we would learn from our siblings in Puerto Rico as hurricanes and floodwaters have once more filled that beautiful island. Once again, the roads are impassable. Once again, their power grid is down, their houses are without power, even though they pay on average 2.5 times what we pay for electricity. They would call out to us and say, "mind the gap."

Here is where Jesus was pointing us. He called us to see the abundance of poverty sitting at our own gates, and the multiple ways we have insulated ourselves from the chasms of suffering around us. Abraham's words haunt us in our haughtiness: a great chasm has been fixed.

Lazarus laid at the other end of that chasm. He was the embodiment of the ones Luke's gospel had repeatedly emphasized: the desperately poor people of the land, who lacked even the basic provisions of life and were dependent on the scraps that fall from the tables of the rich.

And when he died, he was carried into the arms of God's servant Abraham, cared for in ways he never experienced in life. Meanwhile, the rich man also died. But having been comforted by much in this life — and comforted by things that did not really matter — the rich man was sent to Hades.

But even there he failed to see the deep chasm that exists. Even there he still believed he could rely on his privilege and demand that Lazarus bring him water to cool his tongue.

Jesus told us: "Mind the gap."

Anyone familiar with the massive London Underground is familiar with that friendly reminder. It cautions passengers to pay attention to the frequently significant gaps between trains and platforms. The phrase was so popular that during coronation week in 2023, all 2,750 railroad stations across the United Kingdom played recordings of King Charles' greeting to the passengers. The king signed off by adding, "and remember, please mind the gap."[17]

Jesus' parable offers the same reminder—with even more urgency. "Mind the gap," Jesus implied. Those who believe are admonished to remember the ways we become blind to human need. "Mind the gap," and recall the hope of the gospel that God alone has the power to close

17. https://www.reuters.com/world/uk/mind-gap-king-charles-remind-train-travellers-during-coronation-weekend-2023-05-05/

the chasms that separate us. God alone bridges the gaps sin has created, and in the cross of Jesus Christ, God reverses the economic, social, and spiritual gaps that keep us from living as God's holy people.

Ultimately, this parable was about paying attention. It was about noticing that all people are deserving of care. It was a story of how we are called to trust more in God's provision, and less in our own overly embellished sense of importance. It was about believing that while God will act to overcome the gaps of injustice and pain, we are not exempt from acting responsibly toward our siblings.

The good news for us is that Jesus indeed minds the gap. There's no need to be haunted by our own haughtiness. Instead, we are empowered to overcome the gaps we encounter by the humility of Christ's servant love.

This is not a story intended to placate the wounded of our world by reminding them things will one day be better. Nor does it suggest we should be content with solutions to poverty and homelessness that make the wealthy feel better without addressing root causes. The evils of poverty can only be addressed when we begin to "mind the gap," and notice the great chasms that have become fixed around us.

The good news was, and is, that Jesus bridged the gaps. He saw those who others have ignored. He welcomed them, and called all who follow him to preserve the dignity of the Lazarus' of our world. And remember, please mind the gap.

Amen.

Increase Our Faith!

Front porches are the perfect settings for those interminable nuggets of paternalistic comedy more commonly referred to as dad jokes. Depending on your tolerance for dad jokes, they are either winsome and amusing or corny and barely tolerable. Either way, front porches are perhaps the best setting for relaying those predictable puns and obvious punchlines.

I have little doubt that dad jokes were a regular part of Jesus' interactions. Perhaps he didn't tell corny one-liners, but there is certainly compelling evidence that the parables were chockful of incongruities and preposterous images designed to amuse an audience. Father James Martin pointed out overlooking Jesus' hilarity means we're often missing the point of what he was trying to communicate.[18]

As we've already seen, there are plenty of examples of Jesus' humor in the parables. At times it is not hard to imagine Jesus telling stories like Jerry Seinfeld or a homogenized John Mulaney. His stories were filled with eye-rolling details and oversized references that would surely have prompted grins and groans. Read carefully, the parables pick up the background noise of the disciples poking each other in the ribs, or crowds giggling at Jesus' jokes.

But not this week. In Luke 17, Jesus' tone has turned serious. There's no hint of sarcasm in his voice as he challenged the disciples to be bold in upbraiding the sinful and those who cause little ones to sin. Perhaps Jesus was growing weary from the travel to Jerusalem, or maybe his calloused heels have been grinding into his sandals. Whatever, his instructions were filled with harsh words, especially around possessions, and matters of repentance. While earlier chapters were focused on for his opponents, here Jesus shifted his attention toward his own disciples. Today the porch is less of a comedy club and more of a classroom for learning invaluable lessons on leadership, community building, and other details of running a church.

---

18. James Martin, SJ, *Between Heaven and Mirth*, HarperCollins, New York, NY, 2011.

The random series of sayings at the beginning of this chapter may be a clever ruse by Luke. Rather than dismissing these as disconnected chop-a-block aphorisms, it may be wiser to attend to Luke's theological purposes in preparing the church for its witness in the world. Here he seemed to be pointing off the front steps and into the broader horizons of church life, where "occasions for stumbling are bound to come."

The second half of the passage is couched in the language of slavery. Don't negate the impact images of slavery churn up. It's a difficult image and requires thoughtful interpretation on the part of contemporary readers and listeners. Though this passage leaves slavery unquestioned, we do not have that same luxury.

Luke portrayed Jesus giving the disciples a demanding image of faith that is focused, filled with gratitude and motivated to fulfill all the tasks required of disciples. But those are no easy words to swallow, especially for those with a penchant for cataloging the faults of others. Jesus assured the disciples that the world would produce many opportunities for tripping and falling into sin. That presented a sizable challenge. But equally important is the call to forgive those who have repented — even if they have sinned against you every day of the week. As the drama around the porch builds, the questions of whether disciples are up to the task are up for discussion. The closer they got to Jerusalem, the more serious Jesus became.

Porch Talk

I have a habit that makes my wife crazy. Just one.

I have a slight tendency to drive as far as I can go without buying gas. It is somewhat of a challenge for me: just how many more miles can I go until I need to buy gas? Carol, and the other sane members of our family do not appreciate this game. Like most of the world, they prefer to buy gas when the needle goes below half a tank.

In my mind, the tank is never half empty, it's just half full.

She has warned me, however, that I am not to call her if I am ever stranded. I tell her that you need to live by faith — while also reminding her that in 37 years of marriage, I have only run out of gas once. (I did not dare call her.) She reminds me that living by faith does not preclude paying attention.

Because I try to be at least mildly self-aware, I admit she is right. While my mother was still alive, she routinely reminded me that I had inherited the tendency to drive on empty from my father. "You're luckier than he was, and I would suggest you don't press that luck too much!" Point taken: no matter how old you are, your mother's words stick in your mind.

My habit of driving on empty is grounded more in laziness than actual theological doctrine. While I do believe God will provide, I also keep an eye peeled for a Shell station. The disciples, it seems, are engaged in a similar pursuit. Painfully aware that they will soon arrive in Jerusalem, the disciples are beginning to wonder how long their reserves of faith will last. A little, the disciples believe, won't suffice. "A little" means things might dry up. "A little" means they will need to be careful at rationing what is left if they are to fulfill all that Jesus has expected from them. "A little" feels like that dried-up remnant of glue stuck inside the bottle. "A little" won't be enough.

Jesus had plainly warned them there was a rough road ahead for those who believed in him. His warning could not have been more plain: "Occasions for stumbling are bound to come," he told them at the beginning of chapter seventeen, "but woe to anyone by whom they come!" There's no hint of a smile on Jesus' face. Instead, he was all business. He told them that anyone causing a child to stumble would be better off to be thrown into the ocean. He was teaching them practices of arduous, repeated, and frequent forgiveness, perhaps even as often as seven times a day or more. In response, the disciples cried, "Increase our faith!"

They reviewed the tasks Jesus had called them to do and were certain they would not have sufficient faith to get things done. Casting out demons? Feeding the poor? Healing the sick? That would take so much more faith than they had. Proclaiming release to the captives, recovery of sight to the blind, letting the oppressed go free? Ugh. There's no way they had enough for that.

Their faces became filled with fear. It's reminiscent of countless meetings I have had with church boards following the resignation of their pastor. I have frequently been sent by our presbytery to meet with church leaders after their pastor has left. They are confused, scared. One church was even uncertain of how to unlock the doors on Sunday mornings. You can almost hear the murmurings, "Increase our faith!"

Recall that in this passage, Jesus and the disciples were drawing closer to Jerusalem. He filled their minds with constant reminders of the tasks of discipleship. Panicked, the disciples implored him: *give us more*. They were convinced that faith was a commodity that could be stored in excess and doled out little by little. They looked at the obstacles they faced, and they were terrified. There would not be enough.

Around Christmas, 2019, news of a novel respiratory virus affecting China began to circulate in the United States. Most people didn't give it a whole lot of attention. Wuhan, China, after all, is a long way away, and weathering flu outbreaks is commonplace. Within a month, however, the United States was dealing with a growing number of cases of an illness we were then calling the novel coronavirus. Still, few were worried. "We'll be back to normal by Easter," we told ourselves. But by March the bottom fell out. Suddenly, we were facing critical shortages of everything from face masks to toilet paper. Quickly, we moved into isolation mode.

Over the course of a week, our sanctuary was transformed into something that resembled a makeshift television studio. New words like "community spread" and "stay at home orders" entered into everyday conversations.

We wondered, "will we have enough?" Will there be enough resources, energy, resolve…*faith* …to endure whatever would happen in the weeks ahead? Go back to that time and recall how all of us were wondering, "How on earth are we going to manage?"

We certainly understand the disciples' cries. We, too, have pleaded for more faith. We have faced moments when the tiny scraps of faith we hold in our hands simply will not last. The disciples' cries resonate within us because we can well remember the moments when our faith was running on empty. Lord, increase our faith!

A few years ago, my mother passed away at the tender age of 94. She had lived a good life, and while illness had managed to weaken her body, her mind was sharp. My two siblings and I, along with our families, cherished each moment we had with her until she died in January of 2017.

As sad as that was, something more worrisome was happening. We began noticing that our brother, a gifted musician, and educator, was losing many capabilities. Within a few months it became clear he was struggling with some form of dementia, and by the end of 2018 he was living in a memory care facility. Sadly, he died in March 2019.

Just two years after our mother's death, we gathered to grieve my brother's death. *Increase our faith*, I cried to God. *Help us through this time. Remind us that it does not take much more than a mustard seed.*

As sad as that was, our grief deepened as we began noticing that my sister, my only remaining sibling, was also showing signs of Alzheimer's Disease. As her own journey through dementia continued, I prayed over and over, *Increase my faith*. Less than four years after my brother's death, my sister passed away as well.

Lord, increase our faith. Help us to face these extraordinary moments. Give us added measures of grace, peace, and mercy. It feels like our tanks are just about depleted. As a pastor, I know that my story is hardly unique, and that indeed many persons have experienced even more overwhelming grief and tragedy. Each of us remembers the moments when we, too, have cried, "Lord, increase our faith."

In our grief, we look for some way to move forward, only to realize that the options are few. A long time ago, I found myself at the center of a difficult work situation. It was an ugly, painful moment. I remember going for a walk one morning. It was a beautiful spring day, and as I walked, I replayed the conflict in my mind. It seemed hopeless, filled with pain. I walked and I prayed. I contemplated our family's next steps.

"Increase my faith, God," I prayed, "because I'm running on fumes." A little more could make life so much easier. In response, we tend to view faith as a commodity. We bring our shopping bags to church, hoping and praying to have them replenished. We grab whatever we can off the shelves, expecting faith to be like a box of Hamburger Helper. Even a little bit might help us get through this desperate moment.

But notice Jesus' response to the disciples. His words provide little assurance. He first points to a towering mulberry tree and indicates that all the disciples need to relocate it into the sea is faith the size of a tiny mustard seed. Next, he uses the image of slaves bound to menial acts of service as a metaphor for a Christian's life of service. Faith, it seems, is less of a commodity than a daily practice. It takes so little but requires so much.

Instead of pitching them a product or handing them a how-to manual, Jesus instead describes how faith works. He tells them living faithfully is not a matter of relying on a storehouse of some superhuman formula or garnering attention and accolades. Jesus challenges the disciples to understand that living by faith means relying on the super abundance of God's provision. Living by faith means drawing closer to Jerusalem, inch by inch, step by step.

It's not so much a scolding as it is the reminder that they are fearfully and wonderfully made. He tells them they have enough — and even more than that, they *are enough.* His words come as encouragement both to folks who feel the emperor's boot pushing on their necks as well as to twenty-first-century Christians trying to cling to faith in an era of secularism.

Imagine Jesus saying these words with a slightly wry smile. Hear him offering comfort and encouragement to people who have long felt as though they were not good enough, not sufficient enough, or religious enough to live faithfully. Hear them not as harsh critique, but rather as an encouraging invitation. He calls us to cultivate the renewing resources God has already provided.

The question is not "How much faith do we need?" but rather, "What is most important?" What if we have been given all the faith that we need? I wondered about that one night a couple of months ago as I stood next to one of our good friends in the last hours of his life. Steve was a faithful pastor, chaplain, husband, father, grandpa, and friend. His illness had been long and protracted. It would have been easy to give up, to say, "Where can I get more faith for this battle? But Steve's face reflected the grace and peace he had relied on throughout his lifelong relationship with Jesus Christ. Even a tiny seed of that faith could change the world.

Paul shares a similar message to the young church leader Timothy. Paul writes fondly of the sincere faith that lives in Timothy's life — a faith passed to him by his grandmother and mother, and which now forms the core of his life. Timothy did not need more faith — what he had was more than enough to send mulberry trees into the ocean.

It's an invitation to change our perspective, and to discover the treasure in the middle of the orchard. We've been given what we need, and even more. Chaplain Michael Eselun says that in his work with cancer patients, nearly all of them over the years have found a remarkably consistent method for discovering resiliency. He observes patients finding some minute particle of gratitude by noting that "it could be worse."

Eselun continues, "I would say that upwards of 90% of the folks I've seen over the years would make some form of this claim and take comfort in it-- "It could be worse." "I'm just so glad they caught the cancer early." "I'm just glad it hasn't metastasized." "At least I don't have to have radiation." "At least I'm 55 years old and have had a life… look at these kids who get cancer." "I'm glad it's me and not my children." Like I say, it's an effective tool.[19]

In fact, says Eselun, he often fantasizes about how the world may come to an end. He believes that the last human being left alive will take a long slow look around him or her and then say, "Huh…well, I suppose it could be worse!" It's a perfectly natural and sometimes helpful coping response — but it is starkly different than the way Jesus calls us to rely on the potency of pint-sized faith.

Walter Brueggemann observed that "faith in God's promise is a possibility which the world sees as scandalous." Instead of saying, "How can I get more?" faith in God says, "What is most important?"

Amen.

---

19. Michael Eselun, *It Could Be Worse*, from DailyGood.org, https://www.dailygood.org/story/2379/it-could-be-worse-michael-eselun/ (Accessed 9/24/2023).

The Treasure Of Gratitude

There are a few surprises waiting for us on the porch this morning, including both the location and cast of characters of Luke 17:11-19. Luke offered the story of Jesus healing ten lepers and placed it vaguely in an unspecified territory between Samaria and Galilee. One thinks of those old B-grade war movies with rolling titles that read "Somewhere in Europe." The exact location is unclear, but as Fred Craddock wryly reminds, sometimes geography is physical, sometimes literary, and sometimes, theological.[20] There's something to be said about allowing the image of a border zone — a genuine "in between" place that emphasizes the lepers' uncertain status in that society.

While Jesus' destination is certain, his path is somewhat circuitous. We are following the scenic route, apparently. Or perhaps this is a variation of Robert Frost's "Road Not Taken." At any rate, Jesus is crossing borders. He is in a frontier space between Galilee and Samaria which is neither "here nor there." This land between Samaria and Galilee functions a bit like the in-between space provided by a front porch. On the porch, the boundaries between the outside world and private home life are a bit fluid and blurred, a bit like the setting we discover in today's story.

The path Jesus followed leads us straight to a colony of lepers. As it turns out, they were a mixed group of both Samaritans and Jews. This detail was a reminder that Luke's unspecified border setting had greater theological implications, and this too may be surprising. In fact, this story was loaded with surprises: the setting, the people, their interactions with Jesus, and the Samaritan's response to Jesus. Luke stacked these surprises to potentially catch us off guard with a powerful insight about the possibilities of faith. We are surprised by the way a doubly marginalized person manages to seek our Jesus and express his gratitude. The setting and characters become the bread which contain the sandwich of this reminder that all are invited into the kingdom of God, including a Samaritan. Previously, Luke has re-

20. Fred B. Craddock, *Luke*, Interpretation, a Bible Commentary for Teaching and Preaching (Louisville, KY: John Knox Press, 1990), 202.

minded us Samaritans violently rejected Jesus' messengers. Here, we are surprised either by his good manners or by his insights into the power of God at work. Either way, Jesus makes sure the disciples are paying close attention to this surprising porch story.

Another surprise occured as Jesus drew near to the town. Instead of announcing themselves in the usual way, the ten lepers ignored the boundaries placed upon them and shouted for mercy. They dared to cross a social boundary by refusing to yell "Unclean! Unclean!" They implored Jesus, boldly asking for his mercy instead of maintaining strict social distancing. They are eager to meet him, the way so many were eager to return to in person worship during the Covid-19 pandemic. As far as we know, there were no mask mandates in place or gallon-sized jugs of hand sanitizer nearby. These lepers surprise us with their boldness.

Jesus saw them. He ordered them to go and show themselves to the priests, and immediately all ten jumped up and headed out. Along the way, they were surprised to discover that their skin had cleared. We may be less surprised by this, since we can sniff out a healing story a mile away. The effect was flabbergasting, but what happened next was astounding. Ten were healed, but only one took the moment to realize what had happened. Only one was grateful. Only one took time to turn back to say, "Thank you." And that one was a Samaritan.

Surprise, surprise, surprise.

Porch Talk

A couple of years ago, I participated in the ordination service for a young minister who had accepted a calling to be a college minister. His enthusiasm, excitement, and unbridled idealism took me back to my own ordination some thirty years before. He was filled with idealism and joy, leaping to his feet nearly like the lepers summoned by Jesus.

Most importantly, he was filled with gratitude. As a gay man, he was accepting a calling that would have been denied him just a few years earlier. Indeed, many in the church still considered him the way first century Palestine viewed lepers. The contrast to my own journey to ordination could not have been more different. I was blessed by the loving support of my parents, and carried by the prayers of church members. But his family did not attend, and there was no one from the church were he was raised. I had discovered acceptance and affirmation; he struggled to be heard from the sidelines.

Still, his heart was marked by the treasure of gratitude. Like the Samaritan, he had encountered bigotry and exclusion. But also like the Samaritan, he had experienced the warm mercy of God's embrace. God had looked him straight in the eye, telling him to get up and go show himself to the priests.

As I began the sermon, I reminded my young colleague that ministry can be full of surprises — though he likely knew that better than me. Sometimes surprises are good, but many are not so good. Sometimes the surprises are life giving, while others drain every ounce of joy from our spirits. I've come to learn that the trick to these surprises is learning how to embrace life with grace and gratitude.

Grace: discovering the presence of God in standing with a family overwhelmed by grief. Grace: finding the inner fortitude to endure an undeserved tongue lashing from a member offended by another minister's sermon. Grace: being allowed to witness the complexity of an adolescent's emerging faith.

But grace is also gratitude: watching a group of high school students take a few moments to handwrite thank you notes to donors whose generosity had made a trip to a national youth conference possible. Asking them to trade their phones for a pen seemed impossible at first. But their heartfelt expressions of thanks were sincere. The cards revealed how much their lives had been changed.

A collective groan had rippled across the group at first, including my own son! They weren't ungrateful necessarily, just not so motivated to write an actual thank-you card. But then the words started to flow onto the paper, and their hearts were revealed to be as grateful as the Samaritan in today's story.

As I looked at my young colleague that day, I pointed out that ministry, like our own journeys of faith, involves experiencing unmerited grace while learning how to express unexpected gratitude.

This is the heart of the Samaritan's story. He experienced the surprising gift of grace, a grace that reminded him he was unexpectedly included. All of this prompted him to ignore Jesus' instructions. Instead of heading over to the priests, he returned to offer his gratitude. He turned back to say *thank you*, which certainly must have made Jesus' day.

As I said in that sermon, being on the receiving end of that sort of gratitude can be a rare experience in ministry. In my first church, I spent the majority of my time working with youth and their families. That included weekly meetings in a dark corner of the church's basement. It was a place few adults ever ventured, and for good reason. The room was furnished with a broken-down couch that once had been in the office of the former pastor. When it was discovered that the pastor had been having an affair in his office with a local television personality, he was fired, his large office divided into smaller rooms, and the couch hauled off to the basement. The church never understood the strange message of exclusion it was sending to its youth.

They expected the youth to be grateful. Instead, they often felt excluded and ignored, much like lepers whose condition in life rendered them unacceptable. Decades later, it's a safe bet that few of those youth have continued to be church members. Forcing someone to say thank you falls flat, like kids who need to be reminded to say thank you as they dip their hands into a neighbor's trick or treat candy bowl.

What a difference it would have made if, perhaps like Jesus, the church would allow itself to be surprised by the treasures of gratitude which appear unexpectedly. What a difference it would make in our own lives if we, perhaps like the Samaritan, paid attention to moments of grace that catch us off guard.

What was hard about those early years of ministry was discovering that programs, even the most creative and best executed, did not always make room for serendipitous moments of grace and gratitude. Instead, I discovered that the most life-transforming conversations happened outside of that dingy basement. The youth patiently participated in my clever programs. But the real treasures of grace and gratitude emerged during conversations at McDonalds, or in between bites of pizza. Those conversations were often raw and impolite, but also awe-inspiring and wise. Like the Samaritan, they realized something was happening in their lives, and they turned back to say thanks.

That first year in ministry was spent learning how to use the real tools for ministry. I learned that the real tools of ministry may not be worksheets you download, or gimmicks taught at youth ministry conventions. They are, rather, surprising gifts like hope and faith, trust and mercy, love and grace, that are shared freely and without expectation of any return. These are the sorts of gifts the Samaritan invites us to discover. They are gifts God lavishes on us, gifts that cannot be purchased but are rather offered freely, abundantly. They are treasures which grow like apples on trees. They are treasures like grace and gratitude.

After my mother passed away, my sister and I spent some time sorting through piles and piles of family photographs. Some of the people in the pictures are unknown to us, their names only remembered by people who are now gone. In some cases, we relied on little clues from our mother — a Post-It® note with a date and a place, names scribbled on the back of photos, or even a clever bit of rhyme from our father. Those tiny tidbits were often sources of joyful gratitude.

Indeed, the photos are full of gracious memories, of times shared with family and friends. They convey truths about those moments of joy we often miss in the moment. Think about it: how many of the disciples were really paying attention when the Samaritan walked back? It's likely that the power of this story grew as it was remembered and retold.

"Grace and gratitude," wrote Karl Barth, "belong together like heaven and earth. Grace evokes gratitude like the voice an echo. Gratitude follows grace like thunder follows lightning." Yet while we know that gratitude is a powerful force, our world has lost sight of what it means to live as truly grateful people. "The me of gratitude," wrote Diana Butler Bass, "must extend to the 'we' of gratitude as an ethic, a vision of community based on habits and practices of grace and gifts."[21]

Our world needs to rethink the ways it practices gratitude. By that, I mean that we need to learn the practices of gratitude that go deeper and further from merely being polite — though that would not be a bad idea. Jesus pointed to this practice of gratitude, revealing it as a gift that leads toward a new way of seeing, living, being. Luke told us this story to kindle in our hearts the practice of gratitude, reminding us that a life of gratitude is much more than merely saying thanks.

Luke set the scene by making sure we knew Jesus was traveling in this in-between space between Samaria and Galilee. He was in a border space — somewhere between San Diego and Tijuana, or El Paso and Juarez, Detroit, Michigan, and Windsor, Ontario. Jesus maneuvered around this in-between space, and then noticed those ten lepers crying for mercy.

There were ten lepers in the border town Jesus visited. All ten lived apart, obeying the rules which governed people in their condition. They maintained their distance and stayed away. As they heard Jesus approaching, they called to him, crying for mercy.

21. Diana Butler Bass, *Grateful*, (New York, NY: HarperCollins, 2018).

Ten lepers, cast off and partially invisible, made a daring attempt to cross the border that kept them separate. The rest of the village, preoccupied with their normal routines or afraid of being infected, had spent their lives pretending these ten remained invisible.

I'm told that when the actor Anthony Hopkins researched his role as a butler in the movie *The Remains of the Day*, he interviewed a real-life butler for an uber-rich family. The butler told the actor that his primary goal in life is to blend into the milieu of the family so completely that one blends into a room as if one was just a table lamp or a decoration. Hopkins said that one sentence he will never forget is when real butler said that you can sum up an excellent butler in these words: "The room seems emptier when he's in it."[22]

There is a polite nod perhaps, or a mumbled word of thanks, but as the butler fades into the wall, no one ever notices, no one is ever grateful, no one says a word.

As one has said, "that's just the problem with routine ingratitude: it makes people disappear. You are the center of your own universe and others don't warrant entree into that inner sanctum of yourself.[23]"

Ten lepers, sitting at a distance, crying for mercy. They know the rules, and generally try to follow them. But it isn't easy remaining invisible. Sooner or later, something causes one to push beyond the borders that society or others have imposed. Sooner or later, you grow tired of being invisible and just want to be seen.

This story is filled with surprises. It's surprising that Jesus has wandered into this in-between place, it's surprising that the lepers have broken the lawn to shout out to Jesus, it's surprising that they are healed. It's surprising that only one returns to say thank you.

But most of all, it is surprising that Jesus saw them. He did not overlook them or avoid them. "When he saw them," Luke said, "he said to them, "Go and show yourselves to the priests." It's a surprise that they followed his instructions — no smart aleck managed to say, "Gosh, Jesus, we never thought about that before." It's a surprise that he did not heal them. Instead, he told them to fulfill the obligations required by the law.

Surprise, surprise, surprise: they did what he said, and on the way, they were healed.

22. Quote by Cyril Dickman, former butler at Buckingham Palace, quoted by Emma Knightley at the Knightlyemma blog, https://knightleyemma.com/2021/07/14/remains-of-day/, accessed 1/14/2024.

23. https://cep.calvinseminary.edu/sermon-starters/proper-23c-2/?type=the_lectionary_gospel

Jesus said, "Go and show yourselves to the priests." Go and let others see who you are. Get up and go and head back into the mainstream of society. Do not remain on the margins any longer. Follow the surprising invitation of God and see where it takes you.

Ten lepers, crying for mercy. Ten lepers who had been excluded from community. Ten lepers who had spent their lives being bypassed and ignored. All of them run off to the priests. They do exactly what Jesus had told them.

Surprise, surprise, surprise: all of them are made clean. They're no longer invisible. But only one paid attention. And that one was a Samaritan.

Suddenly, one of them looked at his hands, his feet. He touched his face, and felt the smoothness of skin restored to health. He saw that the sores were gone. Ten lepers rushed off to the priests, but only one saw what had happened.

And that one was a Samaritan.

Surprise! Ten lepers were healed, but only one returned to worship God, and to give thanks. Only one saw that he was healed, and that one was a Samaritan. Someone you should avoid at all costs. A foreigner. An immigrant. A gay pastor. A student who shows up in church one Sunday with a name tag that says "My pronouns are 'they' and 'them.'

Jesus' story reminds us that the heart of gratitude is located within our ability to imagine that God is at work in the lives of those we believe are different than ourselves. Ten lepers were healed, but only one saw what had happened.

None of the other gospel writers include this story, which leads me to believe that Luke wants us to know something essential about the surprising nature of gratitude. It shows up in the least likely of places, and then ripples out like ripples on a pond, each wave growing in size and significance.

Gratitude dares to back track. It risks crossing thresholds, and often sees possibilities where others only see differences. Gratitude changes the world by changing us, and by imagining the fresh ways God is about to get involved in the world once more.

Amen.

Proper 24 (29)
Luke 18:1-8

Take This Widow, Please!

Autumn's blaze of colors surrounds the porch this morning, and the air feels a tad cooler. In some cases, there might even be a bit of frost on the pumpkin, to borrow James Whitcomb Riley's words — *Grab a sweater before you head out, and maybe even one of those crocheted chevron blankets your Great Aunt Mary gave you.*

It's time to bundle up, because cooler weather is not the only thing that is chilly on the porch today. Luke 18:1-8 is a tale that blends the coolness of corruption with the even colder brew of injustice. It's another intriguing parable which pairs two memorable characters: a corrupt judge and a persistent widow. Luke sets these characters against a backdrop of the preceding chapter's emphasis on the kingdom to weave a story about the prayer and the certainty that God will grant justice to the oppressed.

This porch tale begins with a stunning contrast between those who seek justice and those, like the evil judge, who neither fear God nor people. Such a judge runs counter to much of what the Hebrew Bible and Jesus have taught. Psalm 94:6, for example, implores God's vengeance against the those who plot to kill widows, while Deuteronomy 10:14-19 upholds God's concern for widows as a description of God's greatness. Earlier in Luke (7:11-17), Jesus has offered compassion to the widow of Nain by raising her only child from the dead.

But such compassion is absent from the cold-blooded judge, whose cruel indifference to the widow's plight is outmatched only by his disregard for God. It's easy to picture him as a diabolical Snidely Whiplash, the archenemy of the old cartoon character Dudley Do-Right. Indeed, the widow's peskiness in hunting him down only adds to the story's comedic edge.

The contrasts are stark: the self-serving judge is pitted against the persistent widow who stalks her opponent until he gives her what she wants. But if the judge is nothing more than a stereotypical scoundrel, what is keeping the woman from being seen merely as a crabby old complainer? If YouTube or TikTok were videoing her pursuit of the judge, she'd likely be called a Karen — an exceptionally nagging and excessively demanding woman featured across social media.

But the judge is not Snidely Whiplash, and the widow is far from the rather unfortunately nicknamed unfortunately nicknamed "Karens" who always seemed to be wanting to talk to a manager. Rather, the punchline of the parable is that we're invited to recall the moments when we have either lost heart or become the soulless embittered judge who has ceased fearing God.

Today, invite both the unjust judge and the persistent widow onto the porch so they can tell their stories. Allow their characters the chance to speak, so that we might discover anew what it means to hold fast to faith, always praying, and never losing heart.

Porch Talk

Sometimes you just don't see what is in front of you. For example, take this widow... *please!* Henny Youngman's old punchline comes to mind as we overhear Jesus' story of the persistent widow and the unjust judge. In fact, it's not terribly hard to imagine Jesus' listeners rolling on the floor, laughing out loud as he regales them with this tale. It is a story that oozes laughter — sort of the perfect mashup of a vintage television sitcom plot merged with contemporary social media's preoccupation with whiny and overindulged "Karens" whose pushy behaviors quickly become viral videos.

But as Jesus drew his listeners into this story, Henny Youngman's cries of "Take this widow, please!" are soon replaced by a deeper message about our ability to trust in the promises of God, no matter how delayed they may be. Jesus' comedic stylings were soon revealed to be something much more substantial. He invited his listeners to understand that prayer is the refusal to yield, a pushing back against the forces which are bent against us.

The powerful judge struts on the scene, outfitted to the nines in a tailored suit and snappy shirt. After a busy morning of hearing cases, he's off to his club for drinks and lunch, and then perhaps to an afternoon of pickleball or quiet studying. He is arrogant and privileged--but even worse, he knows he is arrogant and privileged. He didn't care.

As Luke reminded us, he "neither feared God nor had respect for people."

But just as he headed to lunch, the widow confronts him on the sidewalk. We do not know the details of her case — maybe she slipped on the pavement outside the synagogue, or perhaps she bought a spoiled bird for a sacrifice. Who knows? It does not matter. Instead of giving us a briefing on her lawsuit, Jesus focused on what was and is truly important. Pouncing on the judge, she was incessant in her desire for justice.

Understanding this story means paying attention to what is right in front of you.

In 1979, twenty-year-old Kevin Strickland and two other men were convicted of murdering three people. The other defendants, Kim Adkins and Vincent Bell, both confessed to the murder and also testified that Strickland had nothing to do with the crime. Police had found Strickland's fingerprint on Bell's car but had no other physical evidence. The only eyewitness was pressured to name Strickland, who then spent 43 years in a Missouri prison.

Within a year, the witness recanted her testimony. Thirty-years later, she contacted the Missouri Innocence Project. "I am seeking info on how to help someone that was wrongly accused," she wrote. Meanwhile, Strickland also contacted the Innocence Project. The other two defendants presented sworn statements that he was not with them when the murders happened. Friends petitioned the governor for a pardon. Five federal prosecutors joined with former state prosecutors in calling for Strickland's exoneration. The mayor of Kansas City, Missouri, where the murder occurred, the local prosecutor, and more than a dozen state legislators also joined in seeking justice for Strickland.

But the state attorney general was unmoved. Strickland remained in prison until a court granted him a three-day hearing in 2021. More than a dozen witnesses, including a former Missouri State Supreme Court Justice, testified on Strickland's behalf. Finally, Strickland, now an older man confined to a wheelchair was declared not guilty and ordered release from prison.

Yet the injustices continued: because he was exonerated without DNA evidence, Strickland was not entitled to any compensation from the state for being wrongfully imprisoned. He was released without extra clothing, a state identification card, a bank account, or anything else that would help him succeed.[24]

24. Jesus Jimenez and Claire Fahy, "Missouri Man s Exonerated in 3 Killings After 43 Years in Prison," *New York Times*, November 21, 2021, accessed at https://www.nytimes.com/2021/11/23/us/kevin-strickland-exonerated.html, 11/2/203.

The answer was always in front of the justice system, but they were not paying attention.

In the parable, no one was paying attention to the widow either. She had prayed, and prayed … and prayed. She persisted in pounding against the closed door of injustice. Like Kevin Strickland, no one who had the authority to do something was paying attention. In the end, it was only her persistence that caused the judge to relent. Fearful that her wild punches might give him a black eye, the judge finally agreed.

There she was: the woman he had thrown out of court a month ago, not because her case did not have merit, but only because he was not interested. There she was: the woman who had stalked him down one street and up the next. There she was: the widow who had been trying to get his attention for weeks now. She had been here, there, and everywhere constantly. He was working so hard to ignore her that the facts surrounding her case were lost.

And then: POW! She landed a blow just above the waist. The judge looked pathetic as she chased him around the ring. The crowd was hooked as Jesus kept the story going. Suddenly Jesus' listeners realized this was more than an object lesson on prayer. While the disciples might have first laughed at the incredulous image of a ninety-pound widow chasing a heavy-weight judge all around town, they were suddenly aware the joke was on them.

Suddenly, the disciples saw what was right in front of them. They saw that prayer was more than a mechanical hoisting of requests to heaven, and was instead action that propelled faith forward. "Listen to what the unjust judge says," Jesus told them. "And will not God grant justice to his chosen ones who cry to him day and night?"

Prayer, steady and consistent, pushes through the obstacles. It steadies the hands of those who have been beating their fists against blocked doors of oppression, and abuse. Prayers unanswered and cures delayed mark our existence, but still, we do not lose heart. Two years ago, a teenaged boy in our congregation died as the result of Type 1 Diabetes. His mother, his sisters, his friends, our church, and many others unknown to him hurled their petitions before God. It would have been easy to turn from God and walk away. What some of us encountered, however, was the gift that prayer becomes something more than a cartoonish emoji attached to the bottom of a text message.

And because of it, we did not lose heart. I do not minimize the grief this his family or anyone else, including myself, felt. But I know that God did not delay long in helping us.

My wife and I have been smiling as we have watched our children become parents. When our granddaughter turned two, she emerged into that very appropriate stage of wanting autonomy. Her favorite words at the moment are "no-no-no," which are generally accompanied by an animated swinging of her arms resembling a first base umpire calling a runner safe. When she's not saying "no," she can frequently be heard calling "Momma! Momma!" Our daughter says that happens about fifty times a minute. My wife and I just laugh. "Wait until her vocabulary really develops," my wife tells our daughter. At times I've been known to mutter, "I wonder where she gets that?"

The truth is she is the youngest of a long line of strong, independent women. One of her great-great-great-grandmothers rocked babies aboard a ship sailing from England to America. Another hid with her small children as Union soldiers marched over their farm. Another rode a horse to teach school, even though she could not vote. Her maternal great grandmother was a cancer nurse who prayed for and with her patients, her family, her friends. And when she died, her granddaughters said, "Who will pray for us?"

Indeed, she always prayed and did not lose heart. The widow reminds us that the long slog of faith requires that sort of bold tenacity and unwavering persistence. It requires us to see the promise that is before us, otherwise we will become nothing more than the self-absorbed judge who fears neither God nor anyone else.

It requires bold, feisty, and sometimes even angry prayers that will not let go. Theologian Fred Craddock shared the story of an elderly Black minister, a veteran of so many civil rights battles and fights for justice. The pastor read this parable and then gave a brilliant one-sentence summary: "Until you have stood for years knocking at a locked door, your knuckles bleeding, you do not really know what prayer is."[25]

Amen.

---

25. Fred B. Craddock, *Luke*, Interpretation, a Bible Commentary for Teaching and Preaching (Louisville, KY: John Knox Press, 1990), 210.

Reformed By Humility

Luke 18:9-14 is the second of two parables in the chapter. Both are stories of God's wild, unpredictable grace. It was grace that taught the judge's heart to fear in verse 1-9, and it is grace that teaches disciples the meaning of righteousness in today's pericope. Jesus introduces the parable in verse nine by calling the disciples to be mindful of ways some misinterpret righteousness.

Righteousness is an important theme for Luke. Earlier we were told that Elizabeth and Zechariah are deemed "righteous before God," (2:6) and that the elderly Simeon was "righteous and devout" (2:25). Here Jesus explored what might be called the shadow side of righteousness, the self-righteous who "trust only in themselves." To make his point, Jesus told a story with two very different characters: a Pharisee and a tax-collector.

As noted earlier, it is necessary to avoid falling into the trap of describing Pharisees as stereotypically self-righteous elitists more concerned with fulfilling the words of the law than the spirit. Such tropes lead to antisemitism and reflect an inadequate understanding of Judaism at the time of Jesus and ignore important realities.

The Pharisee's prayer recognized not that he was a particularly holy person, only that he had been zealous in his adherence to the law. If the rules say you can only ring a neighbor's doorbell once for trick or treating, then so be it. This Pharisee was without blemish, and he was certainly vastly superior to the tax collector — a filthy cheat who mingled with Romans and conspired with them to fleece the poor.

If the Pharisee was the nice kid who had been scrupulous about his trick-or-treating habits, then the tax collector was the gangly teenager who was trying hard to look five years younger than he was, and who was likely to throw eggs at your house if you didn't provide him more than one Snickers® bar.

Jesus' words invite us to consider what it means to move through a world filled with both tricks and treats, and to ponder the inscrutable ways of God's mercy. You may believe you have the right answers about faith, and that those unsavory characters who fail to tithe and never volunteer to teach Sunday school have got it all wrong. Yet today's parable offers another view. It's an invitation to consider how the great watchwords of the Protestant Reformation — faith alone, grace alone, Christ alone — are challenging us to see exactly how God is at work.

Porch Talk

The temptation in this familiar parable is to turn the Pharisee into someone he was not. Our eyes see him in all of his prideful, pompous piety, strutting around praising God with mouthfuls of pious self-righteousness: "God, I thank you that I am not like other people: thieves, rogues, adulterers or even this tax collector."

But that robs this parable of its bite, because the truth of the matter is the Pharisee was correct in his assessment. Moreover, he was only rehearsing the liturgy of confession he had learned since he was a young child: what sets us apart is our intention to be holy.

The truth of this parable is its surprise: the one who was most holy, the one who went home justified, the one who understood God's forgiveness was the one who was most like "the other." The one who received mercy was the very one who had withheld mercy, who had been a thief, a rogue, and a cheat.

The Pharisee's struggle was that he had forgotten the beauty of the treasure of humility and grace. He no longer understood the meaning of bold humility.

Today is Reformation Sunday, that Sunday when we recall the bold humility of a German Augustine monk named Martin Luther who defied the prevailing wisdom in disputing the church's interpretation of grace. Luther had no intention of establishing another religion, he merely wanted to do what the prophet Joel imagined in the first reading for today. In Joel, chapter 2, we were invited to dream new dreams of faith. While humility is not generally a term we associate with Martin Luther, he did see his work as nothing more than the tax collector's prayer be merciful to me, a sinner.

That is why we dare to stand to sing "A Mighty Fortress is Our God" on our way out the door today. We go forth, sometimes even sinning boldly, starting by going into the narthex to eat donuts! But we also go forth knowing that even our smallest attempts to serve Christ is an example of righteousness.

Our heritage of faith has wound its way through the centuries until this moment in time when I believe we are once more called to acts of bold humility. To do so means that we take up the posture of the tax collector, fully aware of how we have distanced ourselves from God, and with bold humility pray, "Lord, have mercy."

A few years ago, I had the opportunity to worship with the saints of God at Dexter Avenue/King Memorial Baptist Church in Montgomery, Alabama. Dexter Avenue is one of the oldest African-American churches in Alabama, and is also the church where Reverend Dr. Martin Luther King Jr., served as pastor. Like Wittenberg Castle, Dexter Avenue was also the site of a reformation. It was founded in 1877, in a slave trader's pen and eventually became one of the birthplaces of the modern civil rights movement.

I was in Montgomery with a busload of Presbyterians who were on a pilgrimage to several Civil Rights legacy locations. The center of our weekend was visiting the National Memorial for Peace and Justice, a haunting monument honoring the memory of more than 4,000 persons who were the victims of lynching.

That was on our minds as we were welcomed into the church. Worship was alive and full of energy — which was a good thing because it began at 10:30 and ended promptly two hours later. You have not experienced the power of the Spirit until you have stood and sung, "There's a Sweet, Sweet Spirit in this Place" at Dexter Avenue Baptist Church.You know the sermon is going to go long when the ushers begin passing around paper fans. I would not have been surprised to hear a few Presbyterians among us say, "Lord, I thank you that our church is not like everyone else, including churches with 45-minute sermons."

What struck me that day is that here was an historical congregation that was actually a very typical congregation. It was certainly not a large church, but it was a mighty and gracious community filled with the power of the Holy Spirit as well as the spirit of Dr. Martin Luther King Jr. I do not assume that it was a wealthy church, at least in terms of money. It was blessed with a rich legacy, and was filled with everyday Christians who came to worship, attend Bible study, and plan mission projects. In short, it was like just about any church in America.

Dexter Avenue Baptist was a humble treasure in the orchard of God's kingdom, a landmark where miracles happened. It was a place filled with the story of God; a story that has survived from generation to generation. In those pews, it was not hard to feel the deep assurances promised by Joel in today's Old Testament reading: "I will pour out my spirit on all flesh, your sons and your daughters shall prophesy, your old men shall dream dreams, and your young men shall see visions" (Joel 2:28)

It was humbling to worship in the setting where the saints of God have trod, where others have heard the word proclaimed in power and truth, and to join in praying, "Lord, be merciful to me, a sinner." The jarring reality of standing at the doorway of that great church and noticing monuments to our country's racist past struck me. I realized that not far from where Dr. King shook hands with his parishioners was the Alabama State Capitol where so many laws promoting segregation were written.

I realized that within a hundred yards of where Dr. King preached a message of nonviolent justice there were monuments to a war that had been fought to keep Black people enslaved. "God," I prayed, "be merciful to me, a sinner."

Did I build those monuments? Did I vote for those laws? No, but like the tax collector, generations of my family and so many people who look like me had benefitted from the wealth created by an unjust system. Perhaps that was the message Jesus was conveying as he told this story of two men praying in the temple.

The prayer of the tax collector is a bold, fresh, and unflinchingly humble prayer because it originates in his awareness of God's grace. That is the true treasure that is hidden deep within the orchard. It was that sort of boldness that compelled a monk named Martin Luther to leave his room in the tower filled with the assurance that he was saved by grace. Indeed, it was that same sort of bold, yet humble assurance that called to Dr. King, and that calls to you and to me today. It is that same Spirit that causes us to rise with boldness each week to sing, "Praise God, from whom all blessings flow."

Yet too often we forget just how bold that promise really is.

Last evening, my phone rang. "Chris," the voice said, "this is Steve at Donut Palace. We've had a problem today." Immediately I thought, "There will be an uprising if we do not have donuts on Sunday morning." I gulped hard, and said, "I'm sorry to hear that, Steve. What happened?" Quietly he said, "Our power went out today." I tell you the truth: I was prepared to cancel worship. But without skipping a beat he said, "We value your business, and I'm glad to say we had just enough vanilla glazed donuts to fill your order. Unfortunately, however, you will not have any sprinkled or chocolate donuts today. That's good news, because some of our customers will not be getting any donuts this morning."

Praise be to God! Under my breath, I almost heard myself saying, "God, I thank you that I am not like the other customers at Donut Palace, the gas stations, the convenience stores or even that other church down the street."

That is not, of course, the sort of bold humility we are called to have. Jesus' words guide us back to the dreams of Joel, to the promise of a treasure hidden in the middle of God's orchard: that even though we are no different than anyone else, we are nonetheless made righteous by God's grace.

Let's go back to my trip to Alabama for a moment. I realize that there are plenty of people who might say, "Why would you go visit a museum and memorial that depicts such an ugly, horrible stain on our history? Why experience firsthand the stark horror of more than 4,000 men, women, and children who were denied basic civil rights, refused their constitutional rights to due process and a fair trial, and summarily sentenced to death without even a chance to be arraigned in court?"

Why bother? Why do we bother going to places that are so inherently upsetting? Or why do we bother getting a group together for a mission trip to Puerto Rico? Indeed, why bother with worship at all? Why not stay home, read the paper, watch the game?

Why? Because we are the ones who have glimpsed the joy of orchard's treasure. We are the ones who have found the boldness to pray, "Lord, be merciful to me, a sinner." And we know that moment has changed our lives. We go because we trust in the bold vision of Joel, that God is always creating new dreams of faith.

Last Sunday, as our group was walking through the lynching memorial, I watched as some of the teenage girls who were with us. These young women attend an African American church in St. Louis, MO. As they were walking through the memorial, one of them stopped. The name on the memorial was her family's name. Her fingers ran across the top, and then she said, "I knew I would see my name."

Lord, be merciful to me, a sinner, and change my life that I may act with humility, but also with passion, boldness, and mercy.

I grew up in a suburb of Los Angeles, which was originally the heart of California's citrus industry. But by the time I was a teenager, most of the groves in my hometown had been abandoned or plowed over. Growing subdivisions proved to be more profitable than growing lemons, so as the old saying goes, when life hands you an empty lemon grove, you make money. Before those orchards were cleared, however, sometimes they would sit abandoned for years. Sometimes I would ride my bike into the middle of those untended trees and imagine how those groves might have looked at their peak.

Occasionally, there in the middle of those long-forgotten lemon trees, I would spot a tree that was still producing fruit. It was a surprise, a hidden treasure. Surrounded by old, decaying, and untended trees there would be one that was still growing lemons. Despite all the odds stacked against it, the tree had persevered. Unmanaged and unwatched, it found a way.

I see a glimpse of that sort of treasure hidden growing in the orchards of the church today. It's a treasure rooted in the promises of the prophet Joel and brought to bloom by the parables of Jesus. It is a treasure that calls us to find new purpose by living boldly, yet humbling, declaring the hope God has for us in Jesus Christ.

Amen.

All Saints Sunday
Luke 6:20-31

Blessed Are The Porch Sitters

Remnants of Halloween are skewed across the porch this morning. The street is littered with empty Skittles® wrappers and the guts of smashed pumpkins, while exhausted ghosts and goblins rest from their annual haunting.

Judging by the experience of some young children I know, Halloween is exhausting. Part of this comes the morphing of Halloween from a single day into a month-long season which becomes a lot for toddlers and their parents. By the time Halloween itself rolls around, both parents and children are exhausted from what has felt like an unending series of events, trunk-or-treats, and fall festivals. One parent told me she simply recycled the candy her children had procured from attending various trunk-or-treating events throughout October instead of purchasing new treats. The big night out has expanded into a month-long escapade, and by November 1 there is a longing to rest.

That longing for rest is, in part, what is at the heart of All Saint's Day. While we do not sing, "For all the ghosts, who from their trick-or-treating rest," we do honor the great hope of faith. We gather on the porch today confident the promise of our ultimate rest in faith is assured, no matter how treacherous or fatiguing our journeys have been.

Some Christians quake at the notion celebrating Halloween while others have decided that dabbling in cultural frivolities is not prohibited by Jesus. What seems more important, however, is to remember that just as Halloween was an opportunity for the porch to become a threshold of welcome, All Saints Day also is a moment for hospitality. On this day, we invite the saints of our lives — both big "S" saints and little "s" saints — back to church. We gather with the saints at the thresholds of God's mercy.

All Saints Day calls us to the sacred task of remembering our connections with the church triumphant. In fact, the porch may be a bit crowded today as we jostle around the countless throng of God's holy ones. In this great reunion, we join our hands with the vast communion of saints who have run the race, finished the contest, and whose baptisms are now complete. It is a daunting task, so it is best to plenty of candy corn on hand.

Central to this day is attending to Jesus' sermon on the plain in Luke chapter 6. Luke's shorter version of the Beatitudes would be less familiar to many in the congregation when compared to Matthew's longer version. Here, Jesus captured our attention by describing the immediate impact of living according to God's intent. His words were sparse and compact, offering a focused pronouncement of the meaning of discipleship. His blessings and woes echo the words of Deuteronomy and reveal God's acceptance of the people the world has rejected.[26] We become focused on the realities faced by disciples. The realities of that life included an inverting of the ways the world defined happiness. To those who have left everything to follow him, Jesus said, "Blessed are you who are poor...blessed are you who are hungry now...blessed are you who weep now."

It is as if Luke imagined Jesus standing at the threshold of mercy. He extended an invitation of mercy and welcome, and called the church to its work of welcoming home those whose rest is won. Crossing that threshold means entering that upside-down kingdom where the saints dwell, and where the church presses forward in hope. Here we discover the assurance of Jesus' pastoral promises which are offered to all who dwell within this blessed communion.

The longer I am a pastor, the more I come to appreciate both the poignancy and richness of All Saint's Day. On this day, we give thanks and grieve for those who have gone before us, even as we lean forward to hear "the distant triumph song" that makes hearts brave and strengthens arms.[27]

Porch Talk

There's a photo album in the church office filled with pages and pages of snapshots spanning decades of congregational life. Certainly, most churches have these albums filled with pictures of gangly teenagers from the 1990s with frosted-tipped hair and baggy blue jeans. Flip through these pages, and you'll find photos of the pastor sitting in a dunk tank, choir members rehearsing Easter cantatas, and dozens of rummage sales. Mission trips, work days, Christmas parties—they're all there, held firm in the memories of members and in the hope of God.

26. Luke Timothy Johnson, *Luke*, The Liturgical Press, Collegeville, MN, 1990, pp. 110-111.

27. William Walsham How, "For All The Saints," (1864, public domain.)

Somewhere in our church photos is a happenchance photo snapped on a Sunday years ago. It's framed with simple poignancy: two guys, sitting on the church's patio, sipping coffee and nibbling donuts. If a single photograph could capture a congregation's essence, this would be ours.

It's a pictorial reminder of two saints who rarely missed a Sunday, and who now worship in the church triumphant. We miss them, certainly, but we know they are still with us. They witness to God's unfailing mercy and compassion, and their photo calls us to join them as porch sitters in the kingdom of God.

Jim sat on the left, a lifelong choir member whose big-hearted laughter could rescue even the corniest of preacher jokes. Vernon was next to him, except everyone called him "Cotton" owing to his shock of white hair. Cotton spent his career creating corporate succession plans and his retirement playing as much golf as he could. He excelled at both activities.

Their picture captures them laughing, their spirits delighting in each other's friendship and presence. Yet anyone who knew these men would also know that their lives were not always filled with such free-flowing joy. Neither was immune to hardships or struggle. The joy they experienced in life had been interwoven with painful health crises, job loss, family difficulties, and so much more. But none of that is evident in that simple photograph, which always makes me think of Jesus' words, "Blessed are you who weep now, for you will laugh."

I think of them and imagine them sitting on the front porch of the church triumphant, their hearts lost in wonder and praise. They're joined by other saints I've encountered, too. There was Saint Gordon, patron saint of my middle school Sunday school class. I see Saint Jessie, a tough, yet loving and always wise-cracking woman who served as a wedding coordinator at one church I served. Jessie spent decades guiding bridal parties through the nerve-wracking walks down the aisle.

I see Saint Peggy, a southerner raised in a time of gentility, manners, and oppressive segregation. One day Peggy was running late to a meeting of the local Presbyterian Historical Society. Without double checking the meeting room assignment, she dashed into a conference room and apologized for being late. Unbeknownst to Peggy, she had actually stumbled into a meeting of the Presbytery's anti-racism team. At first, she thought it would be impolite to get up and leave. But as the conversation went on, she began to hear stories she had never heard. She delighted in the friendship she was offered by the committee's Black members and was challenged to enlarge her understanding of privilege and bias. She entered by mistake but left as the newly elected chairwoman of the committee. But she also left changed and challenged by the call to a new and deeper justice.

And now, from her place in the church triumphant, Saint Peggy reminds us of the radical good news entrusted to the church. Her life became a witness to living the reversals Jesus imagines when he blessed the poor, the hungry, the grieving, and pronounced woes on those who have profited from privilege.

When I think of these saints, I see them sitting on God's heavenly front porch, their hearts filled with wisdom and hope, and their bodies freed of the illnesses that had plagued their last days. Freed, their spirits soar toward God — a reminder, as William Walsham How's great hymn says, that "we feebly struggle; they in glory shine." [28]

I look at that picture of Jim and Cotton from time to time, and it gives me hope. Not just a happy memory, but the sort of deeply rooted encouragement offered from recalling those whose race is finished. The picture conveys the silent witness of the countless saints whose witness has shaped the church and whose memory inspires hopeful mission. They are the ones who have fought the good fight, endured the rummage sales, practiced Easter cantatas, and balanced church budgets. They now rest from their labors, praising God with the endless succession of saints.

Their rest is a blessing from God, bestowed on them not because of their success in business or because of the material goods they achieved. They were blessed out of the abundance of God's steadfast mercy, blessed because in this life they gave witness to that hope and showered mercy on the marginalized, poor, and abused of this world.

Luke's presentation of the Beatitudes is firmly rooted in his theology of reversals, which makes an especially poignant text for this day. We remember not only the wealthy benefactors whose gifts built the sanctuary, but those of more modest means who built the church by expending countless hours watching babies, teaching Sunday school, or delivering groceries to the food pantry.

Jesus' words also conveyed a sense of immediacy. He looked across at those whose eyes were filled with the tears of grief, whose bellies

28. "For All the Saints," text by William Walsham How, 1864, in the public domain.

growled for lack of food, whose bank balances were insufficient to pay rent *right then.* He said to those who were currently suffering, "Blessed are you who are hungry *now*…blessed are you who weep *now.*" It is a reminder that though the struggles are long and hard, the promise of God's mercy is near.

These reversals and promises of God's provision enable us to see through our tears. This is the message the saints convey to us, and the hope of their faithful witness. Across ancient canyons of grief, their song reaches our ears so that Jesus' words of assurance are good news to us.

Jesus' words are both familiar and disconcerting to us. We're familiar with the Beatitudes, though perhaps more familiar with Matthew's version. Luke's sermon is shorter, with only four blessings that are paired with four accompanying woes. But while Luke may be short on words, he is long on theology. Indeed, his words are destabilizing in their impact.

They are a curve ball to the comfortable and affluent. They are reminders of Luke's ongoing interests in the poor and marginalized. Instead of adopting Matthew's more "spiritualized" approach (cf. Matthew 5:3, "Blessed are the poor in spirit,") Luke's focus was direct and unswerving. Jesus' sermon in 4:18-21 outlined his prophetic intent: to bring the good news of God directly to the poor and outcast.

Even the sermon's location is different in Luke. In Matthew, Jesus had climbed a mountain while he stood on a level place in Luke, mingling with "those who were troubled with unclean spirits," and all others who sought healing (Luke 6:17-19). Jesus stayed on a level place. That is the essence of his entire message. In Jesus, God was leveling with people, standing among a "great multitude of people from all Judea, Jerusalem, and the coast of Tyre and Sidon." That is our good news, a word of encouragement intended for all of God's people. Those are words of those who are acutely aware of how grief and trauma have shaped their lives.

One of the surprises I have encountered in serving a congregation for many years is the way its life is shaped by grief. "I know why we try to keep the dead alive," wrote author Joan Didion, "we try to keep them alive in order to keep them with us."[29] Didion, who suffered the loss of both her husband and daughter within a close period of time, was expressing what grief counselors call the "continuing bonds" theory of

29. Joan Didion, *The Year of Magical Thinking.* 2005.

bereavement.[30] Put in simple terms, the idea behind continuing bonds is that we will always experience grief over the loss of important relationships. Grief is not a series of tasks to be accomplished or a linear progression toward healing, but as Didion wrote, a process that comes "in waves, paroxysms, sudden apprehensions."[31]

Our own journeys through life are enriched as we recall our continuing bonds with those who have gone before us — Saints like Francis of Assisi, Teresa of Calcutta, and also saints Jim and Cotton of the front porch. We shape our faith by looking at the old snapshots buried in albums, or by recalling the stories of their lives.

We need to hear the stories of the saints on heaven's front porch. We need to consider how Jesus' good news shaped their lives, not just as glimpses of a nostalgic past, but as a call to mission and ministry today. Their stories inspire us to move when the strife is fierce and the battles long. Much more than a yearning for times gone by, the snapshots of those front-porch saints align our hearts to the presence of God in our midst. Their witness reminds us of Christ's presence, and call us to live, as Paul says, to the praise of Christ's glory (Ephesians 1:12).

M. Night Shyamalan's movie *The Sixth Sense* is famous for coining the phrase "I see dead people" some years ago. A young Haley Joel Osment, terrified by the visions he had been having, confided the truth to his therapist, played by Bruce Willis. "I see dead people," the boy said, "walking around like regular people."

While Willis believed he was the therapist, what happened was that Osment became a vehicle for Willis' own transformation. And while I'm not suggesting that the church is haunted this Sunday after Halloween, I am saying that perhaps we ought to try looking for dead people. I believe the church is packed to the brim every Sunday with members of what John Calvin called "the *communio sanctorum.*" The saints, the famous and the ordinary, are all here today. As Calvin wrote in *Book IV of the Institutes*, "unless we are united with all the other members under Christ the head, we can have no hope of the future inheritance."

---

30. Dennis Klass, *Continuing Bonds: New Understandings of Grief* (1996). See also https://what-syourgrief.com/grief-concept-care-continuing-bonds/ for a distilled explanation of Klass' theories.

31. Didion, *Ibid.*

So it is with joy that we welcome those who have gone before us today.

Certainly, there is still work to be done. The hungry need to be fed, the grieving comforted, and the excluded welcomed home. The practical implications of Jesus' blessings and woes lead the church to consider where God is at work in the world. His words challenge the comfortable with the reminder that on God's front porch the poor and the excluded are called to draw near.

But when we sit a while on God's porch, we hear the saints remind us of our calling to extend God's blessing to the world. As Sister Christin Tomy wrote, the front porch is the place where the life of the household meets the life of the world.[32] We see the needs of all who are searching for Jesus.

Up on the porch, we can see the struggling, the lost, and injured. The gospels remind us of the broad swath of people who search for Jesus. Luke told us they included outsiders like the Roman Centurion seeking healing for his daughter as well as many women cured of their infirmities. Up on the porch we find wealthy tax collectors and wounded beggars. His words speak to hearts that are crushed and emptied — no matter their socio-economic background.

Up on the porch, we hear Jesus' words of blessing and experience our continuing bonds with the saints. They tell us, you are enough. You are loved. God is closer to you than you realize.

Amen.

32. Sr. Christin Tomy, OP, https://www.jesuitvolunteers.org/alumni-features/when-front-porches-become-community-spaces, accessed 9/11/2023.

Proper 26 (31)
Luke 19:1-10

Called Out Of The Trees

It's election season, and by standing on the front porch you can see the emblems of our social and political divisions dotting the yards in our neighborhood. As I write this introduction, the 2024 Presidential primary campaign is in full swing, though it seems we live in a time of perpetual campaigning. In a few days, Iowans will march into the bracing chills of winter to gather in the Iowa caucuses.

Yet it is a practice that has become increasingly divisive. That division has been growing for decades, political scientists tell us, noting that a candidate for president in the United States has not garnered more than 53% of the vote since 1984.[33] Some would say that these divisions have always been present, noting that just four times since 1824 has a U.S. presidential candidate received more than 60% of the vote. The last president, by the way, to achieve that was Richard Nixon in 1972.

Some years ago, Parker J. Palmer reflected on the divisions within America and detailed what he called "Five Habits of the Heart" that need to be cultivated if democracy is to succeed. Among them is the notion that we are stronger together than divided, and that it is essential for Americans to embrace the understanding that we are dependent and accountable to one another.[34] He noted that if democracy is going to survive, there needs to be a renewed emphasis on community.

Palmer's reflections are a helpful conversation partner in retelling the story of Zaccheus. We have turned him into a comic book character, but the Zaccheus whom Jesus called down from the trees was much more than that. On the one hand, he was the embodiment of the "other," the person least likely to be named "Citizen of the Year." His wealth had been derived by cheating others, or so we presume, and his career was aligned with advancing the purposes of the forces of occupation. But as his encounter with Jesus revealed, he became the

33. https://www.npr.org/2024/01/13/1224412456/2024-election-american-values, accessed 1/13/2024.

34. Parker J. Palmer, *Healing the Heart of Democracy* (San Francisco, CA, Jossey-Bass, 2011), p. 44.

building block of community. Clearly, this is more than a short story of a pint-sized trickster.

Up on the porch, we can have serious conversations about the things that divide us. We won't be endorsing a particular candidate, of course, but we can speak to the sort of work of reconciliation and salvation promised by Jesus. We can find ourselves either up in the trees or down on the street, in the crowd, or following Jesus. It's a story worthy of our consideration.

Porch Talk

A few years back, a woman we'll call Mrs. Adams called and left a message with a staff member for me to call. The message said she was wondering if I could lead her husband's funeral. That's not an unusual request for me as I am frequently invited to officiate at funerals for people I do not know.

But the next part of the message was peculiar. The staff member wrote that Mrs. Adams said that she and her husband attended our church. That was odd to me because her name was unfamiliar. We didn't have any members or visitors that I cannot recall by that name. Intrigued, I called Mrs. Adams and introduced myself. "Oh, yes, Pastor. Thank you for calling. We go to your church, and I was wondering if you could help with my husband's funeral."

"I'm sure that won't be a problem." I said. "But you have to excuse me. I'm having a hard time recalling you and your husband."

"Oh," she said. "We've never met you, and in fact we've never attended your church," she said. "We're Baptists, though we don't belong to any church right now. Your church is our polling place, and my husband and I always call it *our church*." There, in a nutshell, is the reality of congregational life in twenty-first-century America — the land of the "nones" or those who have no religious preference.

"People are hungry for community," wrote Rebekah Simon-Peter, a leadership coach who has written about the realities facing the post-pandemic church. In her book, *Forging A New Path*, Simon-Peter observed that the aftermath of the pandemic has left people craving spiritual fellowship and connectedness. She suggested that "if we are to emulate Jesus' way, then we must build a true community within the church that is truly spiritual in nature and not merely functional."[35]

35. Rebekah Simon-Peter, *Forging A New Path: Moving the Church Forward in a Post-Pandemic World,* (Knoxville, TN: Market Square Books, 2022, p. 104.

In other words, we need to start thinking like Zaccheaus — a short man with a huge spirit.

Rebekah Simon-Peter's quote and my experience of helping a grieving neighbor came to mind recently as I pulled into the funeral home to do another funeral for someone I did not know. It was covered with motorcycles. Dozens, in fact; most of them expensive-looking Harley Davidson's. "That checks out," I thought, remembering his wife had said to me that her husband had a lot of friends and enjoyed riding motorcycles.

What she did not say was that he was not simply an ordinary motorcycle enthusiast. Rather, he was a member of a motorcycle club. Not a motorcycle community, but a motorcycle club (MC). There's a difference. One is a social club for people who like to ride. The other is a more structured organization most often known by its notorious reputation. Indeed, the guest of honor was not merely a guy who enjoyed riding motorcycles, he was a member of a nationally-known outlaw motorcycle club considered by law enforcement to be a part of organized crime.

My palms began sweating. Clearly, what was about to happen was not going to be a typical run-of-the-mill Presbyterian funeral. Instead, I was going to be standing in front of a whole host of characters, most of whom were wearing motorcycle jackets embroidered with the insignia of the Hell's Angels.

And that was just on one side of the chapel. On the other side, toward the back, were members of a rival motorcycle club. Apparently, this man was so respected within the motorcycle club community that this other club, sworn enemies of the Hell's Angels, were there to pay respect. It was unlike any funeral I have ever led. They were wearing jackets emblazoned with menacing mottos and patches that identified with names like Crazy Al, Weird Mike, Chucky Gutter, Boss Man, and Wildman. One of them had a tattoo that read "Ride free or die."

Clearly, I was in the minority of those present. On the Venn diagram of members of motorcycle gangs and Presbyterians ministers, there are few overlapping lines. Plus, I harbored the strong suspicions that one or more of those attending had served prison time. I wondered where they would be holding the luncheon, but decided I would probably skip it.

The service went fine. Everyone behaved. In fact, if you were listening from outside the chapel you would have thought it was a typical mainline Protestant funeral. Even Wildman gave a respectable eulogy. As far as funerals go, this one was pretty tame.

Afterward, one of the Hell's Angels members came up to me. His eyes were blocked by sunglasses, but I assumed he'd been crying. "Nice job, Reverend," he said, "You did good. Billy was a good man."

His voice cracked, and he looked away, as he fumbled for a cigarette. I shook his hand and thanked him, and then left the funeral home. On the way home, I began wondering if any of them would show up in church the next day, and what it would look like to see the gang members mingling in the narthex following worship. But who am I to imagine how God draws boundaries? Perhaps we have defined church membership in such a way that we would likely exclude people who make us uncomfortable — including a short little guy named Zacchaeus.

Zacchaeus was intent on finding Jesus, but he became unraveled in the process. Everything he had assumed about his position in life was changed by that encounter. It unraveled like a piece of silk, threads falling off the cloth and landing on the ground. This encounter was a reminder that sometimes it takes a good deal of personal unraveling before we can find hope. Perhaps Jesus is reminding us that only when we are unraveled shall we find salvation.[36]

Zacchaeus must have been a natty dresser whose designer blazers were tailored to impress. Yet if you pulled on a loose thread, it's likely his entire garment would become unwoven. It's interesting to compare Zacchaeus to the wealthy ruler Jesus met in chapter 18. Zacchaeus was also wealthy, though as a tax collector his wealth was accumulated in less than reputable ways. He had a lot of money in the bank, but few friends on the street.

When the rich ruler in chapter 18 came to Jesus, he asked what it would take to enter the kingdom of God. He felt he had it made not only because of his prestige, but because of his faithfulness. When Jesus then quizzed him about the commandments, the ruler passed with flying colors. Yet Jesus told him he lacked one thing: he needed to sell his possessions. Jesus instructed him to give all he had to the poor. That was what Jesus believed was the defining mark of fulfilling God's commandments.

36. This sermon is inspired by a worship series, "Unraveled" written and produced by A Sanctified Art, LLC.

It was too much for the rich man, however. He could not imagine doing what Jesus asked and was filled with sadness. Giving away his stuff would be impossible. Jesus seemed to understand that because he told the man (and anyone else), that it would be "easier for a camel to go through the eye of a needle than for someone who was rich to enter the kingdom of God."

The crowd was taken aback. "Who can be saved?" they asked Jesus, who responded, "What is impossible for mortals is possible with God."

Fast forward to the story of Zaccheus. He had heard Jesus was passing through Jericho and was determined to see. As all of us remember, Zaccheus was a wee little man. But his height was no match for his wealth, which was monstrous. As a chief tax collector, old Zach would have been the archenemy of the common person. He would be seen as a collaborator with Rome, and an exploiter of the poor. There's no wonder this pint-sized seeker couldn't get past the crowds in order to see Jesus — they could not stand him.

He may have been a wee little man, but don't confuse that with nice. He was a collaborator with Rome in extracting expensive tariffs and taxes from the working class. He was a cheat and a fraud, despised and hated. Suddenly, the song we learned in Sunday school sounds just a bit quaint.

Suddenly, this is not the story of a jovial comical biblical character played by Danny DeVito. Zacchaeus was seen as a thug, a wretched enemy. He was a squatty little dude who colluded with Caesar and had pushed his way to the top at the expense of others—or so it seemed. No wonder the crowd wouldn't let him see Jesus.

I bet Zacchaeus had been the object of jokes and derision his entire life. Back in school kids probably called him names like "Short-stack Zach," or teased him endlessly by saying things like "Well, I've got to hand it to you, Zacchaeus…since you can't reach it anyway." How short was Zacchaeus? Zacchaeus *was so short* he needed to climb up in a tree just so he could get a glimpse of Jesus.

Coincidentally, hiding in the trees kept him from facing the shame of his lifestyle. It was a most unflattering position. But there he was: caught in the trees, looking for Jesus. He had so much, but none of that had given him VIP access to Jesus, or so it was presumed. Up there, hidden in that tree, all we can see is how desperately poor he was. Up in the trees, he was friendless, alone, ignored, and forgettable.

And that's where the crowd wanted him.

But along came Jesus. Perhaps Zacchaeus had heard the stories about Jesus, how he welcomed sinners and ate with the outcasts. Perhaps he had heard about the ways Jesus had criticized those who accumulated wealth without sharing. Who knows?

What we do know is that while Zacchaeus was stuck in the tree, Jesus came looking for him. He called to Zacchaeus, and demanded that he crawl out of the tree, and then invited himself for dinner. When all the threads of Zacchaeus' life have been unwoven, Jesus showed up.

Remaining in the trees is hard. It's an awkward position because you're likely hiding in plain sight. Yet Jesus saw beyond Zacchaeus' shame and embarrassment. Jesus looked beyond the crowd's attempts to block Zacchaeus from seeing what was happening. It seemed that Jesus saw things others missed.

Indeed, Jesus sees possibilities where we only see dereliction. Jesus remembered that with God all things are possible, where we only find defeat.

Jesus called Zacchaeus out of the trees. He stumbles to the ground, trying to figure out how he was going to tell Mrs. Zacchaeus they were having company for dinner. But then he realized his world had changed. The crowd started to grumble and complain. If a respected, up and coming rabbi was going to start hanging out with cheaters, sinners, and tax collectors, what else could happen? When Zacchaeus stepped out of the trees, his entire world was changed.

Zacchaeus finally found the courage to be comfortable in his own skin. Affirmed by Jesus, he stood on the ground, out of the trees. He was called out of his shame and embarrassment. What was truly amazing, however, was what happened next.

Standing on the ground, Zacchaeus heard the grumbling. He had heard it all before, and he finally found a way to clear his name. He looked at the crowd and looked at Jesus. Then he told them, "Look, half of my possessions, Lord, I will give to the poor; and if I have defrauded anyone of anything, I will pay back four times as much" (Luke 19:8). Once he landed on his feet and was freed from his perch in the trees, Zacchaeus stood his ground.

What is interesting is that some translations translate verse eight a bit differently. Scholars noted that it is possible to render that verse in the present progressive tense of the verb, indicating that Zacchaeus was already donating half of what he owned to the poor. He had found a way for the camel to pass through the eye of the needle. It was just the way he had always done things, and he added to that by promising to pay back anyone he had defrauded. He was no cheat; instead, he was someone who had trusted in God to do what others saw as impossible.

Suddenly, things were not quite what you'd expect—a reminder, as Jesus said, that "the Son of Man came to seek out and to save the lost." This is exactly what Jesus had been doing: healing lepers in the borderlands and eating with tax collectors and sinners. He had been saying this over and over again: "some are last who will be first, and some are first who will be last" (13:30).

Things are not always what you would expect. A biker grieving the loss of his friend. A widowed woman searching for a faith community. A short tax collector longing for acceptance. Nothing is impossible with God.

What happens when you're stuck in the trees, afraid and ashamed? I guess it depends on whether you are looking for Jesus, because we know that he has never stopped looking for us.

Amen.

Proper 27 (32)
Luke 20:27-40

The Questions That Matter Most

To borrow from James Whitcomb Riley, there may be frost on the pumpkin[37] and a bit of chill on the porch today. It's a sure sign that the growing season is ending, a reminder of the changing seasons. Those arriving early to church today may find icy crystals scattered across the lawn, but the air should be warmer when the youth group gathers for its annual touch football classic.

The autumn chill is matched by Jesus' less than friendly reception by the religious authorities in Jerusalem. Ever since his arrival in Jerusalem, they had been watching him closely, quizzing him about his authority, and spying on his activities (20:20). While Jesus remained honest and forthright, the religious elite made no pretense to be honest in their interactions with him.

Jesus' teaching in the temple has both confounded the authorities and left the crowd's spellbound (19:48). The crowd's interest keeps the authorities from seizing Jesus, but their watch continues. Their suspicions mounted, and they continued to look for ways to entrap him. It's clear that silencing him was not going to be particularly easy.

After the scribes and priests have had their turn at Jesus, a group of Sadducees try to nab him in a game of theological gotcha. It's another less than friendly temple interaction between Jesus and the authorities. Ever since his arrival in Jerusalem, they've been baiting traps trying to find a way to stop Jesus from stirring the crowd.

Jesus now stands at the threshold of betrayal, arrest, and execution. Jesus is a marked man, challenged by a parade of spies looking for any sort of charge. They ask him, "Who is it who gave you this authority?" (20:2).

It's tempting to fall prey to stereotypical observations about groups Pharisees and Sadducees rather than paying close attention to the historical realities. It is better to see them as sects organized around certain populist ideas, groups whose intent was to stir their own sort

---

37. James Whitcomb Riley, "When the Frost is on the Punkin" https://www.poetryfoundation.org/poems/44956/when-the-frost-is-on-the-punkin.

of reformation within Judaism. In this case, the Sadducees would be seen as competitors against the Pharisees, so it is unlikely there was any sort of easy collusion between them.

The Sadducees, ("the righteous ones,") were members of the aristocratic classes who yielded power over the temple. As a group, Sadducees rejected any suggestions of the immortality of the soul or resurrection, in contrast to both the Pharisees and Jesus. In his confrontation with hem, Jesus winnows through the extraneous aspects of their arguments, homing in on what is of ultimate importance. Indeed, is there anything of greater importance than resurrection?

Porch Talk

Aromatic pinon wood burns in a firepit near our church's pavilion, which is the closest thing we have to a front porch. It sets the scene for a perfect fall evening. Friends gather, enjoying a succulent fall repast of hot dogs and s'mores — the menu for our traditional "Roast 'Em and Toast 'Em" fall fundraiser for a local food pantry. It's a time of fellowship and "fun" raising, while also raising awareness on meatier subjects.

It's a convivial evening far removed from Jesus' encounter with the Sadducees. Once more he has been cornered while teaching in the temple. The religious leaders have been trying to snare him with big questions about theology and life. Jesus outwits them by sticking to his script and proclaiming God's grace. It's a story we need to hear, a perfect tale for a chilly fall day as the leaves fall to the ground and our minds ponder the promises of God's mercies.

Let's start with the bad news today. If you're sitting in church listening to this sermon, it is highly likely you didn't cash in big on the Powerball drawing last night. If you had, you would have likely been on your way to Aruba instead of worship. Of course, I am also assuming that if you had won, you would have certainly dropped your tithe off at the church on your way to the airport!

The promise of winning it big in the lottery pushes ticket sales. Whenever the jackpot grows big, we begin imagining how our life would change if we won. We start having all sorts of "what if" conversations with ourselves and our friends. Provided you're not taking money away from your family, playing the lottery is likely harmless. It's hardly an investment strategy, however, which leads me to my point: sometimes we are led astray by conversations that simply do not matter.

Which leads me to the good news: God's provision for our lives will be always prove sufficient.

The Sadducees' questions are a distraction from trusting in God's provision. Unlike the Pharisees, the Sadducees did not believe in the resurrection. There's little else known about the Sadducees, and their role in questioning Jesus is unclear. For whatever reason — perhaps in an effort to outshine the Pharisees — they corner Jesus and begin asking questions about a nearly absurd hypothetical issue.

"So, Teacher, suppose a man dies, leaving a wife but no children. According to Moses, the man's brother ought to marry the widow. But say there are seven brothers. When one dies childless, the brother marries the wife. One after another, each of the brothers dies. So, in the "resurrection" who will the woman be married to?"

It's a faulty argument, especially since the Sadducees do not believe in the resurrection. Jesus sees through their attempt to draw him into a larger debate and focuses instead on the question that really matters. He reminds them that the resurrection is not simply a continuation of life in the present but is instead wholly the gift of God. He calls them to remember the appearance of God to Moses in the burning bush, telling them God is not God of the dead, but of the living. Jesus is less concerned about hypothetical debates than he is about proclaiming the abundance of God's provision.

Or, as Justo L. Gonzalez has said, the conditions of the present age won't apply to the coming age of God. The question, "Whose wife will she be?" ignores the radical newness of the coming kingdom. There are many similar questions that have no answer (and that are similar to those that the Corinthians seem to have been asking, and to which Paul responds in 1 Corinthians 15): How old will I look? Will I have a body like that of my youth, or one that looks more like I looked when I died?[38]

Reinhold Niebuhr, in writing about how Christians should understand the final judgment, framed the argument this way. "It is unwise for Christians," said Niebuhr "to claim any knowledge of either the furniture of heaven or the temperature of hell; or to be too certain about any details of the kingdom of God in which history is consummated. But it is prudent to accept the testimony of the heart, which affirms the fear of judgment."[39]

38. Justo L. González, *Luke*, ed. Amy Plantinga Pauw and William C. Placher, *Belief: A Theological Commentary on the Bible* (Louisville, KY: Westminster John Knox Press, 2010), 235.

39. Reinhold Niebuhr, *The Nature and Destiny of Man: Volume II: Human Destiny*, Page 294.

While Luke did not tell us, it is not hard to imagine Jesus rolling his eyes as the Sadducees posed this ridiculous question about a woman married to seven brothers. It's a story filled with more hyperbole than an old Harry Carey broadcast. There's no good answer to a question that is clothed in mystery.

They seem bent on trying to discredit Jesus or promote their own agenda. The problem is, however, they are asking the wrong questions. Jesus, it seems, is asking the questions that truly, ultimately matter — and that is what keeps the crowd spellbound.

Here's what matters: God is a God of the living. God is concerned not with arcane matters of who marries whom in heaven — after all, planning a wedding on earth is hard enough — who is going to pony up for weddings in heaven? The real point, said Jesus, is not how many angels can dance on the head of a pin nor how many husbands this unlucky woman collected. The question they need to be asking is: How does faith challenge our imagination?

The Sadducees weren't known for their rich and varied imaginations. Eventually, they sort of faded into history and disappeared. For whatever reason, both Mark and Luke include this incident in their gospels. There's no clear answer why this story is included, except that perhaps there's a little bit of Sadducee in everyone. Christians wrangle over questions about the resurrection — some want exact details and architectural renderings of heaven while others are stopped by what they perceive as the rational inconsistencies of a man being raised from the dead.

We are, it turns out, all a bit like the Sadducees when it comes to matters of resurrection. Because we are creatures locked in systems of finite time, said David Lose, it is hard for us to comprehend. Jesus pushed those who were asking him questions to think beyond philosophical puzzles to the promises of God that are beyond time. "The claim," wrote Tom Long, is that God raised the fullness of Jesus, the person of Jesus, from the dead. God raised Jesus, the Jesus who was known and experienced in the things he said and did with his body — not the idea of Jesus, not the spirit of Jesus, but Jesus; and that is an embodied reality." [40]

Here, Jesus pushed believers to broaden our capacity to ask questions that matter. Don't worry about pointless arguments, he seemed to

40. Thomas G. Long, *Accompany Them With Singing*, Louisville, KY: Westminster/John Knox Press, 2009, p. 43.

say, but instead consider what it means to be joined with God. Look at the ways God has appeared to Moses. Consider how God has spoken through Abraham, Isaac, Jacob, as well as Sarah, Mary, and Elizabeth. Luke reminded us time and time again that this story of Jesus was built around Mary's simple words: with God nothing is impossible.

The questions that matter drive us back into the story of scripture where we find God forever reaching toward us, inching closer, coming along side, yearning to connect to our deepest needs. Scripture is the story of a loving God who liberates all people from their suffering and anchors our hopes in this promise: "I am the resurrection and the life."

Martin Luther was once asked what he would do if he knew the world was going to end tomorrow. He is said to have responded, "I'd plant a tree." In other words, he would invest in hope. He'd sink his resources into the soil of God's creation, trusting that God will bring about new life in ways that we cannot, on this side of the grave at least, fully understand. The question is not about how many husbands a widow may have had, but rather, "Can God be trusted?"

That is the story we are called to proclaim. That is why our offerings of time, talent, and treasure matter so very much. In making our promises of faith, we are not attempting to raise money. We are, instead, raising hope. "How much money does your church bring in?" is not the right question. The better question is, "What is your church doing to tell the story of Jesus? How are we, as members of the body of Christ, telling the story of resurrection?"

This is our hope. To paraphrase from Tom Long once more, Christians possess not a crudely literalistic faith nor do we "saw off all of death's rough edges," but instead dare to stand together each week and affirm: "I believe in the resurrection of the body."

Our questions, our offerings, our proclamation all lead us to tell stories of hope that release others from their suffering. So often, notes Gil Rendle, in his book "Quietly Courageous," churches fall into cycles of despair and decline by focusing on what he calls "a rehearsal of weakness." Those stories, Rendle said, ask so little of churches, In the hundreds of churches where he has consulted, Rendle notes that decline is always matched with rehearsing the litany of weaknesses. But a story of hope disrupts that vision of decline. That story is one built on faith, and it pushes God's people to stop asking safe questions to pursue resurrection. Step away from those pointless questions, Jesus told us. Don't keep saying "That's not the way we used to do things" but instead guide us to say, "God is not a God of the dead, but of the living."

Amen.

Telling Our Stories

It's almost time to pack up the porch for the season. The days of sitting out front in a sweater are just about over. The signs of the winter are all around: not only are the trees bare, but the neighbors up the street have fled to Florida. Old timers will consult almanacs in an attempt to understand what sort of winter they can expect.

Something similar was happening in the scripture this morning. Jesus was turning his attention from the present to the future. The remainder of the temple discourse in Luke detailed the coming persecution, along with predictions about the destruction of the temple and Jerusalem itself. The foundations were about to be rocked, and the great monuments of this age torn down.

Luke drew heavily on Mark 13 for much of chapter 21, though some of the material is arranged more to Luke's purposes. In particular, Luke avoided mentioning who was posing questions about the temple's grandeur, while Mark named the disciples as Jesus' questioners. We're left wondering who were the "some" who were speaking to him. It evokes images of anonymously submitted complaints about church: "*Some* are saying the coffee is too weak on Sundays," reads a note left on the pastor's desk. "*A few people* are saying your sermons are too long," and so forth.

These anonymous sources address Jesus as teacher, which is often an expression used by non-disciples in Luke. They mystery around their identity reveals their intent in trying to pin Jesus down on what sorts of signs they could expect to show that the end was near.

Apocalyptic themes pop up both at the end of the lectionary year and in the early weeks of Advent. It leaves preachers in a quandary. While many would agree with Ernst Kasemann that "apocalyptic is the mother of all Christian theology,"[41] many feel ill-prepared to deal with these texts, especially when these texts are so frequently misinterpreted or used as theological hammers that split congregations.

---

41. Philip A. Quanbeck II "Preaching Apocalyptic Texts," *Word & World,* Vol. 25, No. 3, Summer 2005, p. 317.

Spending some time reflecting on the way Luke weaves these themes and becoming familiar with his intent will serve the preacher well.

As the winds stir beneath our feet, and signs of potential threats emerge, Jesus urged a calm that evoked his sleeping in the boat while the storm raged. He promised his followers that they would not be left without assistance in telling their stories of faith and added the assurance that "not a hair of your head will perish." (21:18). He invited us to bear testimony to God's faithfulness, and to endure despite all the obstacles. The word that the church hears in the crossfire of anxiety-driven conspiracy theories is that as we face moments of calamity and pain, Jesus pointed us toward the things which endure, reminding us, "I will give your words."

Porch Talk

There was a little bit of family drama playing out at CVS a few nights ago. I had stopped to pick up prescriptions and to get my flu shot. While I was waiting, a father and his grade-school aged daughter were waiting to receive their vaccines. While there was no evidence that the girl was an anti-vaccer, it was clear she was not exactly pro-vaccine, either. The privacy partition could not hide her anxiety and apprehension, and you can believe me when I say I was not eavesdropping. People all the way over in the dairy aisle could hear her protestations.

The girl could scream, and this is from a father who raised three daughters. "Apprehension" is too mild a description. This was all-out fear bordering on hysteria. I was twenty feet away in another aisle trying hard to look like I was comparison shopping baby shampoo. And when the pharmacist brought out the needle, her meltdown was nearly biblical.

Jesus' words in Luke came to mind: "nation will rise against nation, and kingdom against kingdom, there will be great earthquakes and in various places famines and plagues and there will be dreadful portents and great signs from heaven."

At this point, neither her father's calm assurances, nor the pharmacist's appeal to science were proving helpful. The girl vowed that she would rather get the flu and Covid *at the same time* than to get the shot. Her father kept reassuring her, "You do this every time, and it always turns out okay." From my experience, I wanted to tell him that at this point there were only two ways out of his predicament, one of which included promises of copious amounts of ice cream. The other involved a fast immunization technique.

I'm sure you know how the story ends: she got her shots, and the world did not end. After my shot, I saw them over in the ice cream section. Everything was going to be okay.

There's no logical way of explaining to a child that a needle, even a relatively small needle, isn't going to hurt. It's counteruntuitive. Someone holding something sharp lacks the credibility to provide assurances this is not going to hurt. The little girl was smart and had been paying attention to the signs and circumstances around her and had decided this was not going to be a pleasant experience. While it was hardly apocalyptic, her experience was a small example of the way various religious movements over the centuries have paid attention to what Jesus called "these things," and have come to similar conclusions: this is going to hurt. Her only hope was a slight paraphrase of Jesus' words: "By your endurance you will gain Rocky Road."

For centuries, even millennia, followers of Jesus Christ have read these apocalyptic passages of scripture and have become convinced that theirs would be the last generation. In recent years, the most prominent example of this were followers of radio preacher Harold Camping who spent thousands, if not hundreds of thousands of dollars putting up billboards announcing that the world would come to an end at 6 pm on May 21, 2011. In case you were wondering, it didn't happen.

This was an update from some of Camping's earlier prophesies, which included a prediction that the world would end on September 6, 1994. When Jesus did not appear on May 21, 2011, Camping withdrew from the public eye, later begrudgingly admitting that probably no one could ever know when the end of the world would come. (Sidenote: he probably would have saved himself a lot of money had he become a Presbyterian.)

The Bible named these scriptures "apocalyptic," which means "revelation." While we most often think of the book of Revelation, there are many other examples of apocalyptic literature as well, including this chapter from Luke.

A few years ago, a church somewhere made a change to its outdoor sign a few days after Halloween to read, "Jesus is coming. Hopefully before the election." Jesus' concern, however, is not about the outcomes of an election, but rather about the faithfulness of the people of God — a people who are called to offer their witness to the redemption promised by God. We are called to be a people, said Jesus, who anticipate God's coming to us by a faithfulness that persists even when life is most painful and seemingly all hope is lost. It is at those times that hope stands firm. This witness emerges from our testimony about being prepared and standing firm — even when there seems to be no end in sight of our suffering.

The danger is to avoid falling into either a ludicrous literalism or a paralyzed hopelessness, to be diligent without, as Jesus says, being led astray.

I once had a phone call from someone who asked if the church collected food for food pantries. I said we did, and that it could be dropped off at the church during business hours. The person said this situation was a bit different, and that in any case there was much more than they could manage to get to the church. Would it be possible for someone to bring a truck or a van around to their home and pick it up?

Always up for an adventure, I agreed to stop by. What I found were more than a dozen large plastic storage containers stacked along a hallway. Each container held hundreds of pre-packaged dehydrated emergency food supplies, all of it sold be a company whose mission was to help Christians remain prepared for Armageddon. The person said that their late spouse had believed that the world would be coming to an end and wanted to make sure they were prepared.

(Side note: If the world is really coming to an end, I do not think you will need dehydrated food.)

Jesus was aware, however, that calamities, wars, and disasters will always grab attention and make headlines. At times this clamoring for the end of times leads to harmful conclusions like preachers assigning God's judgment to natural disaster. Jesus discounted these false teachers, offering the assurances of hope that the girl in the pharmacy longs for and the apocalyptic preachers can't provide.

Instead, he called upon the disciples to be prepared. Such preparation does not mean carrying around a keynote speech in your hip pocket, or hoarding canned food necessarily, but instead involves one of the most precious aspects of practicing a faith that has been honed by the riches of Christian community.

Chapter 21 began by reminding us that Jesus was paying close attention to what was happening around him. His disciples seemed to be eyeing the temple's ornate stones and rich offerings much like tourists gaping at the Statue of Liberty. But Jesus' eye moved beyond the impermanence of the temple. Instead, as Luke showed, he spied a poor widow maneuvering her way through the crowds. Her tiny, ancient hands clung to two copper pennies. They were all that she had. It is an impossibly meager offering, but with the confidence of one who belongs body and soul not to herself but to God, she flung them into the kettle.

The dull sound they made was the cry of faith. It was this sight that captured Jesus' attention, not the beautiful sanctuary filled with the rich offerings and gleaming artwork. His disciples gawked at the building, their jaws dropped in amazement and awe. But Jesus said: all of this will fade. All of these stones will one day collapse. This will all be reduced to rubble and thrown down.

It's an impossibility that the disciples could not imagine, but also one that rang true for Luke's audience, who were hearing these stories after the temple's destruction. Those who had witnessed the dismantling of the temple were also witnesses to something greater: the life, death, and resurrection of Jesus. This, then, was the story we are compelled to tell one another: by our endurance, we will gain our souls.

For some, this will not be enough. They see these words only as a tale told by previous generations who lacked knowledge of science or reason. For others, the idea of testifying about faith is about as appealing as snitching on the Mafia. Presbyterians well understand this: we would almost always opt for the witness protection program. It's not just that our palms get sweaty out of fear of what we might say. We do not know *what* to say about faith.

We have decided that words like "witnessing" and "testimony" should either remain in the courtroom or be used only in the hands of trained professionals. But it turns out that the stories we tell of faith do not need to be polished gems or even perfectly crafted. Indeed, the promise of Christ here is that we will be given the right words at the right time. We do not need to rehearse a speech, but only be willing to allow others to see the promises we have found to be true. We only need to tell the truth.

Novelist Reynolds Price once said that the world is full of stories, but humans are searching for that one, true, solitary story we can ultimately trust. "While we chatter or listen all our lives in a din of craving," Price wrote, "jokes, anecdotes, novels, dreams, films, plays, songs, half the words of our days — we are satisfied only by the one short tale we feel to be true: history is the will of a just God who knows us."[42]

42. Quoted in Thomas G. Long, *Testimony: Talking Ourselves into Being Christian*, p. 29.

Testimony, Jesus told us, is the story we tell when the world is falling apart all around us.

After I began serving as a volunteer police chaplain, I received new insights into the value of testifying to our faith stories in times of crisis. Not long after I became a chaplain, I received an emergency call to come to the scene of a horrific accident. A young man, just seventeen years old, was walking with two friends along the train tracks near a state park.

Why they were there or what had prompted them to walk along those tracks was unclear. What mattered was that even though he could hear the train approaching, they were unsure of which direction it was coming. Two of the boys were able to get off the tracks, but the third was unable to make it. He was killed instantly.

That was about two hours before I got to the scene. A chaplain's role is to be present. We are called to be witnesses to those who face the most bitter of life's bitter moments. Truthfully, it was an awful scene. But another truth held me that day that I believe held those first responders, and which I pray surrounds that young man's family and friends.

The painful truth of life is that we will be betrayed by things that are familiar to us. Our bodies will fail, our minds may cease to function, we may battle horrible diseases and lose. Jesus promised that not a hair of our heads will perish. Our witness is not shaped by predictions and literalistic interpretations of biblical prophecy, but by the story of the grace of Jesus Christ who stands with each of us in the hardest moments of our lives. That is what I know. And that is my testimony.

Amen.

A Kingdom Of Losers

The porch season has come to an end. The folding chairs are put away, the cushions taken to the basement, and the planters stored in the garage. The season has passed by quickly, but the memories of poignant conversations will linger. Now comes the time to prepare for Christ's coming to us again.

Christ the King/Reign of Christ Sunday is a newbie in the liturgical calendar. Many of us did not grow up in churches where this was observed. Many others are put off by the imagery of monarchs and feudal reigns. It feels a bit like an intruder. For some congregations, a sermon on the passion of Christ so close to Thanksgiving and Advent seems hard to imagine.

The origins of the feast day, however, tell a different story. After World War I, the Catholic church became increasingly concerned with rising tides of nationalism and materialism. The thought was that the rise of powerful nations would lead believers away from understanding the reign of Christ as our ultimate sovereign. While the language is dated in some ways, we know that the impulse toward nationalism remains. This offers a new opportunity to reflect and consider on the questions revealed in Christ's passion story. The interaction between the criminals and Jesus offered a poignant expression of the church's mission to proclaim grace and forgiveness — a mission quite different from the myths of the Savior/nation.

Gathering On The Porch

As you've probably already figured out, there is a bit of strangeness in the way Christians keep track of days and time. You may wonder if I got my holidays switched this morning. It's almost Thanksgiving, a time for pilgrims and pumpkins, a day for football, turkeys, and the occasional strange relative, and here I am reading Luke's account of Jesus' crucifixion. Some of you, I imagine, may wonder if I've lost it. Others of you are certain that I never had it to lose. It is, indeed, quite strange to hear these very Good Friday-and-Easter-sounding scriptures when people are scurrying around getting ready for Thanksgiving and Santa Claus and his reindeer are warming up for their transcontinental flight. I can hear the complaints coming now: it's not even Christmas and now he's rushing us toward Easter?

It does sound strange, and perhaps even a bit jarring, especially for those of us who were raised Protestant and perhaps never heard that the last Sunday before Advent was labeled "Christ the King Sunday." It is, after all, a relative newbie to liturgical celebrations, added just about a hundred years ago.

For those who were not raised in a liturgical church tradition, this notion of "Christ the King" Sunday may be somewhat fuzzy to you. Christ the King Sunday was instituted by Pope Pius XI in 1925 in response to what the Catholic curia observed was a rising tides of secularism and nationalism. Looking over the wreckage of World War I, Pius was concerned that the world would continue to become more secular, more divided. In his words, "As long as individuals and states refuse to submit to the rule of our Savior there would be no really hopeful prospect of a lasting peace between nations."[43]

As more and more churches began adopting the Revised Common Lectionary, Christ the King or Reign of Christ Sunday became part of the church calendar. It marks the end of the church year, giving the church an opportunity to think again about our allegiance to Christ before we plunge head long into the season of Advent. We call it "Christ the King," or "Reign of Christ," which may sound unfamiliar but are better than the name used by Swedish Lutherans who call this the "Sunday of Doom."

Sunday of Doom sounds more like the title of a Marvel® comic book movie than a liturgical celebration. It's a bit overstated, perhaps, but theologically not far from what we proclaim on this day. Christ the King Sunday offers a timeless reminder that the kingdom of God extends beyond any earthly kingdom — beyond consumerism and secularism, beyond all political ideology, beyond all sociological formations.

It offers us a concrete sign of our hope in Christ. That hope secures our lives in times of struggle and pain, no matter if that struggle comes from the doomsday of airport delays, rising tides of secularism,

43. "Quas Primas," Encyclical of Pope Pius XI on the Feast of Christ the King," (1925), accessed at https://www.vatican.va/content/pius-xi/en/encyclicals/documents/hf_p-xi_enc_11121925_quas-primas.html, (10/7/24).

climate change, or unrelenting racism. Whatever the kingdom of this world may be, it rarely emerges from hope and truth.

Indeed, there are few signs of hope near the crosses on Golgotha. What we do find is yet another stunning use of Luke's mastery of reversal. This has been his theme throughout the gospel. Things are not always what they may seem to be: those who are rich are actually poor; those who are sick are healed; those who are excluded and marginalized are honored. So it was as the executioner's party arrived at Golgotha.

There were three crosses that day, two set aside for criminals who had been justly condemned, and one set aside for Christ. "Two others," Luke reminded us, "who were criminals, were led away to be put to death with him. When they came to the place that is called the Skull, they crucified Jesus there with the criminals, one on his right and one on his left."

Next comes the bargaining. If you're condemned and having nothing to lose, why not try shout out at God? "If you are the Messiah," cried one of the criminals, "Save yourself and us!" Nothing like placing your bets on self-preservation! The other guy, however, was moved by Jesus' lack of sin. He wasn't motivated by selfish power, and had perhaps already sensed the way that God works in the world. Perhaps he had perceived that God's kingdom breaks into the world not through acts of power, but through sacrifice, humility, and repentance. breaking into the world—not through acts of power, but through humility, and repentance.

"We are getting what we deserved," the other said. "But this man has done nothing wrong." And he said, "Jesus, remember me when you come into your kingdom."

There is our king: not a privileged leader, but a suffering servant. Over a generation ago, the Presbyterian theologian Shirley Guthrie Jr. wrote "words like lord, ruler, king, and kingdom sound strange to us. They sound so archaic, so undemocratic — —and so male!"[44] His point is well taken. Afterall, we are the ancestors of the colonists who kicked the king out of America. Guthrie continued, however, to remind us that when it comes to describing the action of Christ on the cross, few words are adequate. As Luke reminded us, Christ's gruesome cruci-

---

44. "Shirley C. Guthrie, "Christian Doctrine," (Louisville, KY: Westminster/John Knox Press, 2018), p. 276.

fixion is not the assassination of a political leader, nor the martyr for a crusade, nor the impeachment of an elected representative.

It is the death of the one who brought good news to the poor, proclaimed release to the captives, and set free the oppressed. Jesus continued to defy expectations. As his life on earth was ending, he brought compassion even to the repentant thief. Here was our king: gasping, choking, yet filled with mercy as he prayed, "Forgive them." To those who are able to see the way God is at work, he said, "Today you will be with me in paradise."

Christ *is* our Lord, our king. We use this language carefully to help us understand that as king he is not a ruler who demanded that his tea be brewed to a precise temperature. Nor did Jesus expect that his pajamas would be pressed in the evening and his shoelaces ironed in the morning — as, apparently, it has been rumored that King Charles III expected. Rather, in his crucifixion and resurrection, Jesus had become the Lord of God's kingdom—a kingdom of love, justice, mercy, and above all else forgiveness.

And God's kingdom — the kingdom that we fervently pray will come — is both a future ideal and a present reality. That is the vision we are given. Again, to quote Shirley Guthrie, "To be a Christian is to get to work to make the ideal a reality."

We strive for this kingdom. We pray for the strength to make it happen. We pray for the grace to forgive as Christ forgave — a forgiveness that goes well beyond forgiving your aunt or cousin for not making Thanksgiving dressing strictly according to grandma's recipe.

It may seem odd to hear this story so close to our celebrations of Advent and Christmas, but it offers us the reminder of what we are called to do and who we are called to be as followers of Christ. Jesus, crucified on the cross, was the child born out of scandal. Jesus at Golgotha is the same Jesus of Bethlehem, whose birth as a king was heralded by choirs of angels and groups of smelly, hard scrapple shepherds.

Jesus, our king, was born for this. We survey the wondrous cross and see it for what it is: the last, futile gasps of earthly kingdoms and powers to render God impotent and weak. Crying with a loud voice, Jesus does not yield himself to those powers, but to an even greater power: "Father, into your hands I commend my spirit."

It is an astonishing moment, a holy moment. It is a reminder that in the suffering of the Son of Man we see glimpses of our own moments of torture and struggle. We know that God's love is not a love reserved for only the pure, but rather extends from the cross into the depth of pain and rejection.

But in this moment, we dare to try and look two directions at once, just as the repentant did. Today, with Advent just around the corner, we dare to look toward the coming of Christ in the baby who will be born. But in the dying figure of Christ, we dare to make another affirmation: Christ has come, and Christ will come again.

Such an affirmation is more than a matter of nodding our heads in agreement to faith or a doctrine worked out centuries before our birth. This affirmation of Christ as King resonates within our own lived experiences of the faith. This is what we hear when we listen carefully to the story of his crucifixion. Luke's moment by moment depiction of the crucifixion slows the action. Suddenly the distinct differences between the kingdoms of this world and the kingdom of Christ emerge in all of their stark differences.

It is by hearing this story that the church becomes more like Christ, and that you and I discover what it means to be part of a kingdom of forgiveness.

It is also a moment of holy possibility, a chance for us to see what we are called to be and do as Christians. There, rejected by all, God's love is offered anew. "Thy kingdom come," we pray, as if we really know what we're saying. To pray for that kingdom is to invite God's grace to reshape us — as well as the church — to be part of the kingdom of forgiveness.

Forgiveness is hard. It is risky. It takes shape in ways that challenge us to do what seems impossible. Those sorts of bold and controversial acts, modelled after Christ's own forgiveness, catch off guard. Following the 2015 shooting at Mother Emmanuel AME Church in Charleston, South Carolina, some of the survivors and family members attended the arraignment of the shooter. He was a young, deranged white supremacist who exchanged the welcome he received at the church door for vicious, cold-blooded murder.

Yet, when some of the survivors attended the arraignment, they did what many could never imagine doing. As the shooter looked at family members of the victims, he heard Nadine Collier, the daughter of one of the victims say, "I just want everybody to know, to you, I forgive you. You took something very precious away from me. I will never talk to her ever again. I will never be able to hold her again. But

I forgive you and have mercy on your soul. You hurt me. You hurt a lot of people. But God forgives you. And I forgive you."

Wait, what?

Of course, such forgiveness is not always possible nor perhaps advisable. It is clearly not easy. It's also important to understand that not all the families were able to forgive, either then or now. But Nadine Collier did not forgive him to waive away the pain or to erase the suffering he caused. She did it as a witness that the cross brings changes we cannot fully understand. She offered testimony to Christ her king.

Christ is king — but not a king crowned in an ancient cathedral with choirs singing and lords and ladies adorned with robes and coronets. Christ is a king whose coronation takes place between two thieves, and whose reign is marked by forgiveness, peace, healing, and justice.

"It is clear," said Walter Brueggeman "that dominant culture in North America no longer knows what time it is, because every season has now been homogenized into an uninterrupted 'shopping season' and when we do not know what time it is we are unlikely to remember 'former times' and surely have no ground to hope for 'new things'." It is, he said, only when we pay attention to the church's seasons that we understand that the emptiness of the "timelessness of consumerism" is replaced by possibilities of "the timeliness of our faith."[45]

The consumerism and materialism that drives so much of our lives is propped up by the kingdoms of this world that push us to do more, have more, buy more. This is consumerism's timeless reminder. Yet the kingdom of God — the kingdom of Christ — is a reminder that our ultimate satisfaction, our deepest sense of wholeness, emerges from something as ugly and yet timely as Christ's crucifixion.

Remember that old song from the band "Chicago?" Does anyone really know what time it is? Does anyone really care?" It is the time of the kingdom of Christ.

Amen.

---

45. See https://christiancalendar.squarespace.com/

Thanksgiving Day
John 6:25-35, Deuteronomy 26:1-11

No Expiration Date

Jesus challenged the crowds to search for bread that did not perish, the bread that gives life to the world.

It was a few days before Thanksgiving, my freshman year of college. Ronald Reagan had just been elected president by promising supply-side economics and a restoration of American military strength. At the same time, however, rising tides of inflation and poverty were making it difficult for many families to survive. Within a few months, nearly 32 million Americans, or about one out of seven, were living beneath the poverty line.[46]

Politics was far from my mind, however. I was focused on surviving my first semester of college, packing up my room, and getting home. While I was attending a college in my hometown, the dorms would still be closing the next day and I had a pile of clothes screaming to be washed. Before I could tend to that, however, my mother called to remind me that I was supposed to help my father with our church's meal distribution.

I rushed out of class and popped into my sleek 1978 Ford Fairmont — a preacher's car if there ever was one. Up at church, I found my dad helping a local minister load boxes of food into a pickup. Reverend Garcia, a pastor of a local Latino congregation, helped us distribute the food our church had donated. Years later, I now realize that while these sorts of programs are always well intended, they also create problems.

I wasn't sure why my help was needed. Dad and Reverend Garcia had managed to pack up the truck before I got there, and everything seemed to be ready to go. But then Dad grabbed my shoulder and said, "Chris, hop in the truck and go with Osvaldo. Help him with the deliveries." And off we went.

Within minutes, I was standing in a world I did not know existed. My college was within walking distance. You could see the outlines of

---

46. See https://www.census.gov/library/publications/1982/demo/p60-134.html, accessed 9/17/2023.

the dining hall, a room I knew was packed at that moment with hundreds of students complaining about the food. Meanwhile, I turned toward this tiny house and carried bags of groceries inside. The family had more children than food. The kids laughed and giggled as I struggled to haul in a frozen turkey, along with bags of rice and beans. Reverend Garcia spoke to the mother, who dabbed her eyes.

I realized why my dad decided I needed to deliver the food with Reverend Garcia. It was my own "best of times/worst of times," moment. A football field and some classrooms stood between this family that had nothing and a room full of 18–22-year-olds who were griping about the turkey cutlets and trying to steal extra desserts. (Dining hall turkey was never good, by the way, but that's a different story.) The contrast was stunning and is an image I recall every year at Thanksgiving.

It is a sacred story, not unlike the story of God's people entering the promised land, or Jesus feeding the five thousand. It was a moment of discovering the presence of God amidst the hungers of life. It became a profound moment of learning about the various hungers we all experience — the hunger of the child who had nothing in his belly; the hunger of college students despite an abundance of provisions; my own hunger to participate in the spiritual body of Christ.

In John, Jesus' frustration with the disciples' hungers was becoming palpable. Obviously, they had seen him break the bread, and share the fish. They saw how a little boy's lunch fed more than five thousand. But that was yesterday, and today they were hungry again. Maybe not a physical hunger, but certainly a yearning to see more of this man's amazing miracles. There was a hunger that even the miraculous, ever-multiplying loaves could not fill, and so they were on the hunt for Jesus.

Today's scripture continues the conversation Jesus had with the crowds he fed in the wilderness. They were looking for him, but Jesus knew that it was only because of the bread had given them. He reminded them of that, and told them they were actually hungering for something different.

Whenever my grandmother would come visit, my father would only make one request: please make some bread. I realize there are families whose grandmothers possess amazing culinary talents. I have been told about grandmothers whose recipes were legendary, passed from generation to generation. I have even heard about grandfathers who make amazing pancakes or succulent barbecue.

My father never asked his mother to cook a meal. Grandma Keating was many things, but she was not a cook. In her home, the green beans and the beef roast for Sunday dinner were both put on at the same time, and both served four hours later. If it is possible to cook things beyond well done, then Grandma had that perfected.

But what she could do was bake: bread, especially, but also cookies and cakes and pies. Coming home from school when grandma visited was like walking into an amazing bakery. The warm, fresh inviting smell of bread welcomed you. I understand how the crowd had eaten their fill of bread one day and had come back wanting more because I could never get enough of grandma's bread.

John focused our attention on the crowd's pursuit of Jesus. But Jesus knew they were only interested in the bread he gave. The crowd had witnessed the sign he performed, but they did not understand it to be anything more than an astounding picnic lunch. He challenged them, "Do not work for the food that perishes, but for the food that endures for eternal life."

Jesus, in John's gospel, was not ignoring the crowd's physical hunger. He was more than willing to satisfy their growling stomachs. But Jesus was also focused on probing the deeper spiritual hungers — those hungers that exist in all of us:

Hungers to be accepted. Hungers to be welcomed and loved. Hungers to abide in the presence of God who never leaves us wanting. Hungers to see something astonishing, like the miracle Jesus worked with the little boy's lunch.

In response, Jesus engaged the crowd in an amazing conversation, exhorting them to labor for bread that had no expiration date. John's tactic here was to have Jesus express explicitly what the other gospels inferred or left implicit. He saw beyond their impatient needs for something to eat here and now and put before them the bread that would feed them for all eternity.

Hunger will always return, even after we have filled ourselves at the never-ending cruise-ship sized buffets the world puts before us. We can fill ourselves on all the empty calories of sweet tasting food and perfectly roasted meat, but eventually those hungers return. Jesus was determined to help the crowd understand that there is bread which does not rot or spoil, and which provides a deeper sense of satisfaction.

"Whoever comes to me will never be hungry," Jesus tells them. He will be the bread which remains, and it is our relationship to Jesus which sustains and satisfies the restless, ever-churning longing within each of us.

"You have made us for yourself, O Lord," prayed Augustine, "and our heart is restless until it finds its rest in you."

Fifty or so years ago, most Presbyterian churches withheld communion from children until they were confirmed in what was called "communicant's class." But that policy was changed, officially when I was seven or eight years old. Presbyterians began allowing children to receive communion, which prompted my parents to bring up the subject in the car one Sunday. We were riding to church — cars are always the best vehicles for theological conversation — and my parents took time to explain communion the best they could. This was no regular meal, they told me. It was the meal Jesus shared with the disciples. It was bread, yes, and ordinary grape juice, to be sure. But it was also a sign of belonging to God in Jesus Christ. My parents were no theologians, and I have little memory of exactly what they said. I am equally sure my parents were glad that I didn't ask a lot of questions — but really, what questions would I have asked? Communion always exhausts our explanations. I needed to experience it.

Not long afterward, we attended another church while visiting relatives out of state. As the elders were passing the communion trays, I reached out to take the bread. But the elder reached beyond me, giving the tray to my father instead. My dad looked at the man, looked at me, and offered me the bread.

There was something in me at age nine that wanted to give the elder a lesson on church polity, but my father just told me to take the bread and be quiet. There is within us a hunger for the bread that does not perish.

Years later, my friends and I discovered that the best part of communion happened in the church kitchen after worship. On communion Sundays, we'd gather around as our parents cleaned up the communion ware, eager to get some of the leftover bread and drink some of the left-over grape juice.

That was what it meant to taste the bread that does not perish. I've been thinking a lot about how our world hungers for the bread that does not perish. Disciples were called by Jesus to share our material bread, of course, and we do that by taking care of the poor and fragile. We make sure that the hungry are filled with good things. But there are deeper hungers that are not so easily satisfied. As we have moved out of the isolation and difficulties of COVID, we know those sorts of hunger pangs all too well.

John focused our attention on the way Jesus had come to us. Throughout the gospel, Jesus was revealed through miraculous signs: water that was transformed into wine, people who were healed, a woman called to quench her thirst with the water of life, and crowds fed with bread and fishes. Jesus used ordinary elements of water, wine, bread, and touch to reveal the love of God for the world. He came to bring the gift of abundance, meeting people in their needs while revealing the presence of God in human flesh.

At each moment, Jesus was pointing not to himself, but the love that God has for the world.

But the crowds did not yet understand. They clamored after him because of the miracles. They sought Jesus the way some people seek out a new restaurant, anxious to see if what their friends said was true. "He gave them bread," someone said, while another added, "Oh, man, was that bread great!" And then another said, "I want some bread," and another added, "Yeah, I want more of that bread." Pretty soon the entire crowd is worked up about bread — bread that was not just good, but great. Even better than great — sacred, holy, unimaginable.

They found Jesus and immediately began asking where he had been. They had been looking for him, though Jesus knew they were only interested in the free bread. They had tasted the bread of heaven, and they wanted some more.

As far as they're concerned, the miracle here is that Jesus fed them. They were in a lost and lonely place, lacking resources and in need of nourishment, and Jesus fed them. They had made a big mistake, and sometimes we make the very same mistake.

Jesus turned their attention to the deeper hungers of life, the sorts of hungers that are not satisfied by bread. He engaged them in a conversation, trying to help them realize the meaning of the loaves and the fishes. They enjoyed the feeling of being satisfied but failed to understand that there is another sort of satisfaction, a feeling of being loved and accepted, a knowledge that you are held deep within the provision of God.

They did not understand. They were fixated on one thing: where to get bread to eat. They were like hungry teenagers descending on their parent's kitchen late at night: they knew there was bread someplace, so Jesus let them have that bread. And he gave it to us right then.

There is a longing within each of us for a religion of convenience that will make us feel good, give us the answers we want. We want the spectacular delivered to us with all the bells and whistles.

There is, or was, a Mexican restaurant in Denver that was known less for its food than it was for its spectacular shows. The entire restaurant felt like a Mexican village. There were divers who dove from fake cliffs into pools of water. Mariachi musicians strolled by tables, and puppet shows entertained kids. They did not worry about the authenticity of their recipes: food was served quickly, cafeteria style.

The show mattered more than the substance.

The crowds clamoring around Jesus were impressed by the miracle, but they weren't interested in the one who provided the abundance. They loved the bread but were not especially interested in the relationship. They yearned for the feeling of being full — Lord, give us this bread always! — but had little interest in the one who was offering them the bread of life, the water that would quench all thirst, the hope that would raise us to new and eternal life.

Author Sara Miles was raised in an atheist home. She lived the first 46 years of her life in a thoroughly secular way, and had no religious connections at all. But one day she wandered into a church. It was, she said, "for no earthly reason. I was certainly not interested in becoming a Christian, or as I thought of it rather less politely, a religious nut."

But then she ate a piece of bread, and took a sip of wine. "A routine activity for tens of millions of Americans," she writes. And to her great astonishment, that bit of bread and sip of wine turned out to be more than a mere symbol: it became to her the bread of life.[47]

"There's a hunger beyond food that's expressed in food," Miles writes, "and that's why feeding is always a kind of miracle."

Passing the bread and cup, Sara Miles suddenly realized that her deep spiritual hungers would only be met as she fed others. She returned to that church the next Sunday, and the Sunday after that. Not long afterward, she organized a food pantry in the church. Once a week, church members would place the food they had donated in bags

47. See Sara Miles, *Take This Bread*.

on top of the communion table in the sanctuary. Then they opened the doors and began feeding their neighbors.

Her words tell the story best. "I was, as the prophet said, hungering and thirsting for righteousness. I found it at the eternal and material core of Christianity: body, blood, bread, and wine, poured out freely, shared by all." There, on the table where she first met Jesus, she was sharing bread with the hungry.

When Jesus said, "I am the bread that has come down from heaven," he directed us beyond the miracle to the one whose abundance never ceases, whose care for us never ends, whose desire to love all in the world is boundless. And unlike the manna that fed God's people in the wilderness, this bread feeds us forever, bringing us the gifts of eternal life.

Theologian Ronald Byars said that if this sounds too good to be true — and it does for many of us — "then let it be taken both as a promissory note and also as a state of being that does in fact lift us, transform us, and gain a foothold in us now and then." [48]

"I am the bread of life," Jesus told them. "Whoever comes to me will never be hungry, and whoever believes in me will never be thirsty." Stop looking for the magical bread. Stop trying to find quick fixes. Look instead for that bread which never goes bad, which does not have an expiration date. The bread that endures.

Jesus offered them a relationship. He offered himself, just as God provided manna in the wilderness. It was not Moses who tap-danced his way into feeding the people, but rather God. It was God's grace who guided them, who fed them, providing not exactly what we want but precisely what we need. In one of her books, Barbara Brown Taylor put it this way, "God provides exactly what we need: some bread, some love, some breath, some wine, a relationship with this ordinary looking man who comes from heaven to bring life to the world." The crowds did not understand all of what he said, and at times we may not either. But here is bread, here is wine. Let's eat and discover together the promise that does not perish.

Amen.

48. Ronald Byars, *The Sacraments in Biblical Perspective.*

www.ingramcontent.com/pod-product-compliance
Lightning Source LLC
Chambersburg PA
CBHW031145090426
42738CB00008B/1222